WHERE TO GO AND WHAT TO DO WITH THE KIDS IN SAN FRANCISCO

by Mary and Richard D. Lewis

PRICE/STERN/SLOAN
Publishers, Inc., Los Angeles

Second Printing, May 1974

Copyright ©1972, 1974 Price/Stern/Sloan Publishers, Inc.
Published by Price/Stern/Sloan Publishers, Inc.
410 North La Cienega Boulevard, Los Angeles, California, 90048
Printed in the United States of America. All rights reserved.
Library of Congress Catalog Card Number: 72-76841
ISBN: 0-8431-0189-X

FOREWORD

This book is dedicated to our grandson, George Maxfield Hunter, but it was written for all parents, grandparents, youth group leaders, and harassed out-of-towners whose youngsters ask, "What are we going to do today?"

We hope this book will provide a lot of good answers.

We have tried to select from a great variety of places and activities (many of them free) those that would be of most interest to kids. If we have missed something you think should have been included — a camp, tour, exhibit, class or special attraction — please write and tell us about it. We'll be glad to consider it for future editions.

Please note that hours and prices are subject to change. All were correct as this book went to press but to avoid any possible disappointment, it would be best to double-check them by telephone before starting out.

San Francisco is a great place for walking. Public transportation — buses, street cars, ferries, and cable cars — will take you anywhere in the City, to most places in Berkeley or Oakland, and to many other places in the Bay Area. As this book goes to press, BART (Bay Area Rapid Transit) is operating the 37-mile run from Richmond through Oakland to Fremont, the 17-mile line from Concord to Oakland, and the line from San Francisco and Daly City (17 miles). The link under the Bay is now scheduled for operation late in 1974. Until then the trains run on weekdays only. BART has been plagued by many problems, but when it is operating at full efficiency, it will prove a fast and efficient method of transportation. (See page 144 for more information and phone numbers.)

Directions for getting places by BART are given for all areas in the East Bay which can be reached by train directly or with A/C connecting buses. If no bus lines are mentioned, you are within easy walking distance. Information about Muni line connections to BART stations in San Francisco were not available at press time. We recommend that you telephone the appropriate transportation agency for routes and time schedules.

The authors acknowledge with thanks the cooperation of the places included in this book, and wish to express their appreciation to the San Francisco Convention and Visitors Bureau for assisting with a number of the illustrations.

There are several major developments and many lesser ones pending at press time, which would greatly expand recreational facilities and wildlife areas in the San Francisco Bay Area. These include establishment of the Golden Gate Headlands Park, expansion of the Point Reyes National Seashore, and development of San Pablo Reservoir as a public fishing area.

CONTENTS

OUTDOOR ADVENTURES　　7

Summer and winter trips for the whole family or special fun just for young people. Everything from beachcombing, biking, camping, skiing and sailing, to ferry rides and white water rafting.

CHILDREN'S CONCERTS, FILMS, TV & THEATER　　35

Culture for the kids — the kind that makes them ask for more. Music, films and theater specially planned for their level and enjoyment, plus opera, plays and puppet shows. Even Shakespeare made easy.

FREE TOURS　　45

Eye-popping and educational tours through everything from a bakery and ice cream manufactory (with samples) to a heliport, cable-car barn, fireboat and police station.

MUSEUMS, OBSERVATORIES AND PLANETARIUMS WITH SPECIAL ATTRACTIONS FOR KIDS　　61

Every sort . . . guaranteed to delight a child and surreptitiously add knowledge to his resisting noggin.

VERY SPECIAL BIRTHDAY PARTIES   75

Ideas for successful parties for preschoolers to sophisticated teenagers. Clowns and magic, special birthday facilities, hayrides or a far-out catered dinner with groovy entertainment provided by a professional party planner.

CLASSES TO DEVELOP TALENTS AND HOBBIES   87

Something for everyone. Art, astronomy, auto mechanics, sports, sailing, ceramics, cooking, film animation, horseback riding, ice hockey, music, singing and dance — and more.

ORGANIZATIONS   111

Whatever your child's interests, these groups provide friends and facilities to expand his knowledge.

WHERE TO TAKE OUT-OF-TOWN VISITORS AND THEIR KIDS   121

Now's your chance to visit all the lovely touristy places that you've needed an excuse to go to — amusement parks, wax museums, harbor tours, Marine World and The Mystery House.

MISCELLANY   137

Some facinating odds and ends including some possible places for young people to get jobs, cable car routes and how to get bus and street-car information and maps.

CALENDAR OF EVENTS   145

What goes on month by month around the Bay, plus some special events not too far outside the city, of interest to the whole family.

ABALONE PICKING — The Marin-Sonoma coastline offers some of the best shore-picking of abalone in the state, especially at Tomales Point and between Fort Ross to Stewarts Point. Abalones can still be found in good numbers during minus low tide at rocky areas along this coast. Skin divers will find red abalones in nearly all rocky areas from Bodega Bay to Gualala and on Tomales Point. A flat prying bar, not over 36 inches in length, is the preferred method for removing abalone from the rocks and bring an accurate measuring device. Limit: five abalone. Minimum size for red abalone is 7 inches; green, pink or white, 6 inches; black, 5 inches; all others, 4 inches. Undersized abalone must be replaced immediately, with the shell outward, on the surface of the rock from which detached. Pickers over 16 must have a fishing license. Season: March 16 through January 14.

AQUATIC PARK (Beach Street at the foot of Polk Street, San Francisco, 885-2177) is a public park with swimming and fishing off the municipal pier. Nearby are the Maritime Museum, anchored historic sailing ships which can be boarded, and Fisherman's Wharf. Lifeguard on duty summers, 10 am to 6 pm.

Directions: Polk Street north to Beach Street.

AQUATIC PARK (foot of Addison and Bancroft Streets, Berkeley) includes a nature area and bird refuge, picnic areas, rowing, sailing and water-skiing. Learn-to-Sail classes are conducted from March through November (minimum age 10 years). For classes or sailboat rentals, phone John Beery, 845-6310.

Directions: Any BART Berkeley station and AC 65 bus. By car, Highway 80 north to University Avenue exit. Take first right to 2nd Street which runs into park.

BEACHCOMBING — The San Francisco area abounds in beaches where kids can pick up unusual stones and shells at low tide, observe small creatures in rock pools, and collect driftwood.

AGATE BEACH (Marin County) is rough and rocky with two pincer-like reefs stretching seaward, once a graveyard of ships. At ebb tide there are wonderful pools filled with tiny fish, crabs and other small animals.

Directions: Highway 101 across Golden Gate Bridge to Highway 1. Just before Bolinas, take Elm Road to beach.

FORT CRONKHITE BEACH, facing San Francisco across the Golden Gate, has a smooth pebble beach, with multi-colored stones for rock hounds. A short way up the beach, Bird Island, a great rocky mass reached only at low tide, rises from the water. Marvelous beachcombing here also.

Directions: Highway 101 over Golden Gate Bridge; take first off-ramp to Bunker Road, through Barry-Baker tunnel to Rodeo Lagoon.

The beaches at **PESCADERO** and **ARROYO DE LOS FRIJOLES**, down the peninsula (south of San Francisco, along Highway 1), have tidepools, shells and driftwood.

PEBBLE BEACH is noted for its treasures of agate, jasper, and other colored stones. There is no swimming at any of these.

BEACHES — Swimming is prohibited at most San Francisco Bay Area beaches because of extremely dangerous coastal undertows or because of pollution. Swimming is permitted at ocean beaches only where a lifeguard is on duty. Check water conditions before setting out. (San Francisco Health Department, 558-6345.)

ALAMEDA BEACH (620 A Central Avenue, Alameda, 531-9300) fronts on San Francisco Bay bordering the island city of Alameda ("place where poplars grow"). There are picnic areas, swimming and wading, sunbathing, fishing along its two miles of beach. A large turfed area adds to the attractiveness as do the summer nature programs for youngsters conducted in its "Old Wharf" classroom. In June, there's an annual sand castle contest, with three entry categories: family; groups of 11-year-olds or above; groups of 10-year-olds and under. Three hours are given to complete the sculpture and judging is on the basis of design, detail, neatness, and technique. Fun either to join in or watch. Phone for date.

Directions: BART Fruitvale Station and AC 64 bus. By car, Highway 17 south to Jackson Street off ramp, then through Webster Street Tube to Central Avenue.

OCEAN BEACH (on Great Highway), San Francisco's most accessible surf beach, is a long, clean beach that's good for picnicking, wading, and building sand castles. It's also a good place for shells, colored stones, and occasional fossil sand dollars at low tide. Free.

Directions: Take Fulton Street west to the ocean.

PARADISE BEACH COUNTY PARK (east shore of Tiburon peninsula, 479-1100) has a pier to fish from, picnic facilities, swimming, but no lifeguard. The park is open from 6 am to 9 pm and is free.

Directions: Highway 101, across Golden Gate Bridge to Paradise Drive off-ramp, to the beach.

DRAKE'S BEACH is on the bay Sir Francis Drake thought was San Francisco Bay when he landed here in 1579, and it still remains very much as it looked in those days. It is believed that white cliffs behind the beach reminded Drake of Dover and for this reason he called the land New Albion. White rolling sand dunes and rock pools filled with tiny marine creatures make Drake's Beach special for kids. There's swimming (when lifeguard is on duty) and picnicking. Free.

Directions: Highway 101, across Golden Gate Bridge to Highway 1; take to Sir Francis Drake Boulevard, turn off on Drake's Beach Road and follow it to the end.

CHINA BEACH (James D. Phelan State Park, between the Presidio and Lincoln Park) is the only San Francisco beach safe for swimming, but the water is very cold, as elsewhere. A lifeguard is on duty summers from 10 am to 6 pm. Free.

Directions: Geary Boulevard to 25th Avenue, turn right to El Camino del Mar, turn left to park.

STINSON BEACH (on the Marin coast) is a family resort with a three-mile white sand beach with picnic areas and lifeguards on duty during summer months. Boats, tackle and bait are available for surf fishing. Open 9 am to 6 pm winter; 9 am to 10 pm summer. Admission: 75 cents per car; $3 per bus.

Directions: Highway 101 across Golden Gate Bridge to Sausalito turnoff, then Highway 1 to beach.

POINT REYES NATIONAL SEASHORE (Point Reyes, 663-1092) provides grasslands, wild flowers in the spring, 10 miles of white beach, hiking, beachcombing and surf fishing. No swimming or wading here, as the undertow is extremely dangerous. A beautiful, if windy, area in the early spring from which to watch the gray whales migrating north to the Bering Sea. There's picnicking and fires may be built in the concrete rims. Open throughout the year. Free.

Directions: Highway 101 north to Sir Francis Drake Boulevard exit, west to Olema, and take indicated roads to either Point Reyes Beach North or Point Reyes Beach South.

BICYCLE RENTALS — Around Golden Gate Park bicycles can be rented from the following cyclery rental shops: Stanyan Cyclery, 672 Stanyan Street, 221-7211; Fischer's Bicycle Shop, 640 Stanyan Street, 751-6617; Wheels Unlimited, 772 Stanyan Street, 387-5115; Kezar Cyclery, 854 Stanyan Street, 751-4726; Lincoln Cyclery, 4621 Lincoln Way, 664-3459. In Marin County, Mill Valley Cyclery, 369 Miller Avenue, 388-6774.

Directions: Take Fulton Street west from Civic Center to Stanyon Street. Turn left to Waller Street and the bicycle shops are along the next three blocks. Turn right on Lincoln Way for the Lincoln Cyclery. For Mill Valley, take Highway 101 north. Miller Avenue runs through the center of town.

TRIPARK BIKEWAYS are made up of a 7½-mile bikeway through Golden Gate Park, with a 3½-mile bicycle trail to Lake Merced and a proposed 5½-mile trail through the Presidio to the Golden Gate Bridge. The bikeway through the park passes the Conservatory, MacLaren Rhododendron Dell, and several lakes. For sport cycling enthusiasts, a banked oval track encircles the Polo Field — a fun place to watch if your bicycling skills aren't good enough to ride it yet. Call San Francisco Recreation and Park Department, 558-3706, for free map with bike safety rules and inspection chart.

MARIN COUNTY PARK AND RECREATION DEPARTMENT (Civic Center, San Rafael, 479-1100) will furnish a map of 11 bike routes, two of which cross the Golden Gate Bridge. One links up with the Tripark Bikeway and the other runs down the Embarcadero (heavily trafficked by trucks and cars on workdays) to the Ferry Building. One of the best and most rewarding for children is the Bear Valley Trail, 10 miles round trip, starting at Olema Park headquarters, off Highway 1, where cars can be parked and free trail maps are available. The rolling, *unpaved* trail, winding through grassy meadows and forests, open to hikers and bikers only, ends with a breathtaking view of the ocean. No food or drink available, so bring your own.

Directions: Follow Highway 101 north to the Marin County Civic Center off-ramp on North San Pedro Road.

SAUSALITO PARKS AND RECREATION COMMISSION (530 Nevada Street, Sausalito, 332-1837) sponsors a teen center which a teen director keeps open, organizing bicycle rides and trips to Angel Island, along with other activities for young people.

Directions: Highway 101 across Golden Gate Bridge, take Sausalito off-ramp. Follow Bridgeway to Bee Street.

LAKE CHABOT (Oakland-San Leandro area) has a scenic bicycle trail which runs along the varied shoreline of the 315-acre lake in Anthony Chabot Regional Park.

Directions: Cross Bay Bridge; take MacArthur Freeway (Highway 580) to Dutton Avenue-Estudillo off ramp, turn left onto MacArthur Boulevard and left again at Estudillo Avenue which becomes Lake Chabot Road. Continue to Marina entrance.

BOATING. The largest lake in Golden Gate Park, STOW LAKE (752-0347) encircles an island called Strawberry Hill. Rowboats, electric motorboats and fastback boats may be rented at the boathouse. The lake is populated by numerous waterfowl. Picnicking across the bridge on the top of Strawberry Hill (no tables or benches) or on tables by the lake near the boathouse. Children under 12 must be accompanied by an adult. Open Tuesday through Saturday, 9 am to 5 pm; Sunday 9 am to 4 pm. Closed Mondays, except for holidays. Food is available at snack bar, 9 am to 5 pm.

Directions: West on Fell Street to John F. Kennedy Drive in Golden Gate Park.

LAKE MERRITT (Lakeside Park, Oakland) has sailboats, canoes, and rowboats for rent as well as an excursion boat for a summertime cruise to points of interest around the lake (adults, 40 cents; children, 25 cents). Sailboat races are a popular feature in spring, summer and fall.

Directions: BART 19th Street station. By car, Highway 580 to Grand Avenue exit, turn right to Bellevue Avenue, left to boat house.

LAKE TEMESCAL (6500 Broadway, Oakland, 531-9300) has boats for rent, fishing, a sandy beach, bath house and swimming June through September with lifeguard on duty. There are a children's play area, hiking trails, and picnic facilities. Free. Food service available.

Directions: BART 19th Street station and AC 59 bus. By car, Highway 580 to Highway 24; exit at Warren Freeway intersection, and follow signs to the lake.

CAMPGROUNDS AND CAMPING.

San Francisco Recreation and Park Department (558-4971, 558-5031) for boys and girls 7 through 12 years of age. **SILVER TREE CAMP** in Glen Park Canyon and **PINE LAKE CAMP** in Stern Grove cost $4 per week, for meals, transportation and activities, Monday through Friday, June to August. Activities include hiking, cookouts, nature study, music, storytelling, crafts, fishing and swimming. Registration is at neighborhood playgrounds and quotas are limited, so call for registration date.

BERKELEY RECREATION AND PARKS DEPARTMENT (Berkeley Camps Office, 1835 Allston Way, Berkeley, 644-6520) sponsors Camp Woodland, a day camp at Tilden Regional Park, July 6 through August 23, for boys and girls 7 through 12 years of age. Costs are $5 for five days and cover transportation, milk, and insurance. Campers bring daily lunch. Activities include hiking, picnics, exploration of lakes and nature areas, crafts, cookouts, campfire programs. Supervised by carefully selected staff. Signups begin first weekday in April at Berkeley Camps Office. Limited space, so register early.

Directions: Walk west from BART Berkeley station. By car, Highway 80 north to University Avenue exit, turn right on Grove Street and right on Allston Way.

CAMP MATHER (Tuolumne County, 558-4870) is maintained by the San Francisco Recreation and Parks Department for family camping. It is situated on the middle fork of the Tuolumne River, below Hetch-Hetchy Reservoir (elevation 5,600 feet). Free brochure detailing cost, accommodations, and other information will be mailed on request.

ECHO LAKE CAMP (near Lake Tahoe) and **TUOLUMNE CAMP** (near Yosemite Valley) for family overnight camping are maintained by the City of Berkeley (Camps Division, 644-6520). Tents, cabins. Hearty meals are served family style. Hot showers and laundry facilities are available. Activities include fishing, boating, hiking, swimming in heated pools, organized games and crafts for children, dances and moonlight hikes for teenagers. Camp open July 1, closes August 31. Very modest rates include three meals and lodging. Reservations may be made any time after January 1.

BOOTJACK and **PAN TOLL CAMPGROUNDS** (Mt. Tamalpais State Park, Marin County) are steep and rocky but have stoves, water and toilets. They are beautifully located, and the view from Mt. Tamalpais is exceptional. Camping is $1 per day per car. Pan Toll has a ranger station.

Directions: Highway 101 across Golden Gate Bridge to Highway 1 to Panoramic Highway.

POINT REYES NATIONAL SEASHORE (Point Reyes, 94956) maintains four camps: Coast Camp, Sky Camp, Glen Camp, and Wildcat Group Camp (6 sites for organized groups). Access is by trail only, and camping permits are required. The first three camps have 12 sites each, with water and toilet, and each has a limited stay of one night per camp. Call 663-1092 for reservations. For additional information, write to the Superintendent, Point Reyes.

Directions: Cross the Golden Gate Bridge and take Highway 1 to Olema. Superintendent Headquarters are one mile west of Olema on the Bear Valley Road. There is parking here, and Valley Trail and Sky Trail, both of which lead into the Coast Trail, begin here.

ANTHONY CHABOT REGIONAL PARK (Oakland-San Leandro, 531-9300), with 4,740 acres, offers picnic and youth group camping areas, as well as family camp area.

Golf course, archery and motorcycle area also.

Directions: MacArthur Freeway to 35th avenue turnoff (East Oakland). Left on 35th toward hills, becomes Redwood Road. Continue on Redwood to intersection of Skyline and Redwood. Stay on Redwood 6.3 miles to Marciel Gate entrance to park.

FRIENDS OF THE HIGH SIERRA (2526 Shattuck Avenue, Berkeley, 849-2567) conducts three summer sessions of backpacking in the High Sierra, July 7-21, July 28-August 11, and August 18 to September 1, for high school aged campers 12-17. Cost to camper, $130 per two-week session. Some scholarships are available. Six experienced hike leaders provide an invaluable introduction to wilderness living, campcraft and nature lore. Contact Friends for details and early application as only 17 campers are enrolled each session.

YOUNG MEN'S CHRISTIAN ASSOCIATIONS of the Bay Area (S.F., 885-0460; Marin, 472-1301; Oakland, 879-0223; Berkeley, 848-6800) sponsors summer day camps, overnight camps, hikes, river trips, fishing expeditions and backpack trips. One branch accepts boys as young as 5, but the usual ages are 6 to 18. There are day camps for the 6- to 11-year olds (one- or two-week sessions, about $15 a week, child returns home each evening) and mini camps (two days and one night). For the 8 to 12 age groups — boys, girls, and coed — there are three-day hikes, canoe and fishing trips (about $19). For teens, there are one-week trips to the High Sierras, Carlsberg Wilderness, Mt. Lassen, the gold country, and a six-day trip by raft down the Rogue River in Oregon, through wild water canyons, camping at night on the river bank. Fees for these trips, though modest, vary from branch to branch, so call your nearest Y for information. The Marin Y goes even farther afield, with a coed (age 16 to 21) Peruvian Work Camp, from the end of July to September, fee $795.

CLAM DIGGING. The California Department of Fish and Game (411 Burgess Drive, Menlo Park, 415-326-0324) will supply you with information on the best times and tides for clamming. Since clams live under the surface of the sand, the best utensils for uncovering them are a shovel, rake, trowel or garden fork. Work down or dig about until you hit something hard, then get underneath it and lift it out.

In Northern California, Pismo clamming is best in the Moss Landing-Watsonville area. The limit is 10 clams, at least five inches in diameter. Smaller clams must be reburied at once, hinge side up. Washington clams and gapers (limit 10, no minimum size) and Littleneck (limit 50, minimum size 1½ inches) can be found at Tomales Bay and Dillon Beach. Bolinas Lagoon was a good clamming ground before pollution forced its quarantine. This may be lifted some time in the future, so check if you're interested in the area. A fishing license is required for all areas if you're older than 16.

FERRIES: San Francisco residents and visitors are fortunate that the ferries have been restored. They are a great thrill for children and even the ferry commuter never tires of the magnificent views of the city, bay, surrounding hills, and passing boats.

GOLDEN GATE FERRY (Golden Gate Bridge, Highway and Transportation District, Millie Dunshee, 346-5858) runs 11 times a day, weekdays, and 8 times a day, weekends and holidays from the San Francisco Ferry Building, Pier 1, to downtown Sausalito. Complete schedules available from Bridge District. Snack bar serves hotdogs, apple turnovers, soft drinks, and other kids' favorites. Rates for the 30-minute ride: adults, 75 cents; children, 6 to 12, 25 cents; two children, 5 and under, free with adult. For those taking the ferry from Marin to the city, there is convenient free parking north of the ferry dock.

Directions: Take Van Ness Avenue south to Mission Street. Turn left to the Embarcadero and then left, past the Ferry Building, to Pier 1.

ANGEL ISLAND-SAN FRANCISCO FERRY (Harbor Carriers, Inc., Pier 43, S.F., 398-1141). This ferry, from Fisherman's Wharf to Angel Island, started as a warm weather service but became so popular that it's now a year round activity. Minimum of four sailings every Saturday, Sunday, and holidays. Daily service June 1 through September 10. Time is 45 minutes each way. Fare is: adults, $1.75 round trip; children 5 to 11, $1, under 5, free. Prices subject to change for 1974.

TIBURON-SAN FRANCISCO FERRY (Harbor Carriers, Inc., Pier 41, S.F., 398-1141) runs weekdays to either the Ferry Building or Fisherman's Wharf and weekends and holidays from the Wharf only. Fares: one way, 80 cents; round trip, $1.50; children under 5, free. Prices subject to change for 1974.

Directions: Pier 43 is at the end of Powell Street. Take Van Ness Avenue north to Bay Street, turn right to Powell, then left.

TIBURON-ANGEL ISLAND FERRY (Angel Island Ferry Service, 21 Main Street, Tiburon, 435-1094) leaves from the Main Street dock daily during summer months only, weekends and holidays all year round. Fares: adults, $1.50 round trip; children 5 to 14, 75 cents round trip; children under 5 free.

Directions: Cross the Golden Gate Bridge on 101, turn right on Tiburon Boulevard. Main Street crosses it at the water's edge.

BERKELEY-TIBURON-ANGEL ISLAND FERRY (Harbor Carriers, Inc. 398-1141) sails from Berkeley to Angel Island and Tiburon once a day, Saturdays, Sundays and holidays only, 9:30 am, from April through October. The time each way is about one hour. Angel Island fares: adult round trip, $2.25, children, 5 through 11, $1.25. Tiburon fares: adult round trip, $2.75; children, 5 through 11, $1.40.

Directions: BART Berkeley Station and AC 51 M bus. By car, Highway 80 north to the University Avenue off ramp. Turn left at the top of the ramp to the Marina.

FISHING. A popular fishing spot for young and old San Franciscans is the Muni Pier (Beach Street, S.F.). No fishing license is required here. The view and salt air are fine. It's also possible to catch sand dabs, perch, ling cod or, if you're lucky, bass or salmon.

Directions: Polk Street north to Beach Street.

LAKE MERCED (Skyline Boulevard and Harding Road, S.F., 556-0300) is not far from the ocean, covers about five acres and is fed by fresh-water springs. There is trout fishing on the Children's Pontoon (with a lifeguard in the summer, 10 am to 5 pm). Small sailboats are for rent at the boathouse. A short walk will take you to neighboring Fleischhacker Zoo.

Directions: Fulton Street west to Park-Presidio Boulevard, left through Golden Gate Park into 19th Avenue, right on Sloat Boulevard to Skyline Boulevard to Harding Road.

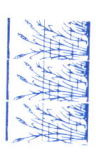

BERKELEY MARINA on San Francisco Bay (end of University Avenue, 644-6371) provides fishing, sailing, cruising, sun-bathing on sandy beaches. It includes a restaurant and cafe. The fishing pier extends 3,000 feet into the Bay and is open daily free of charge. No fishing license required. Sportfishing boats are for hire every day (Bait and Tackle Shop, 849-4615), and will go as far as the Farralones, if you wish.

Directions: BART Berkeley Station and AC 51 M bus. By car, Highway 80 to University Avenue off ramp, turn left over the freeway.

EAST BAY REGIONAL PARKS DISTRICT (11500 Skyline Boulevard, Oakland, 531-9300) operates more than 30,000 acres of rolling hills and meadowland dotted with lakes and watered by streams. The parks are open year round, free. The lakes are stocked with bass, carp, and rainbow trout, and there is fishing at Anthony Chabot, Cull, Temescal, Del Valle, Don Castro, Contra Loma and Shadow Cliffs Parks. A state fishing license and a $2 District permit are required for fishermen 16 years or older. All lakes have picnic grounds nearby. Rental boats, bait, tackle and food service are available. Call the District for a map of the area and a brochure describing the parks' facilities.

Lake Chabot has an annual fishing derby in mid-August, with prizes for the biggest fish caught, a casting contest, and other jollities. The contests are divided into two classes: 15-year-olds and younger, and 16-year-olds and older. The prizes include rods and reels.

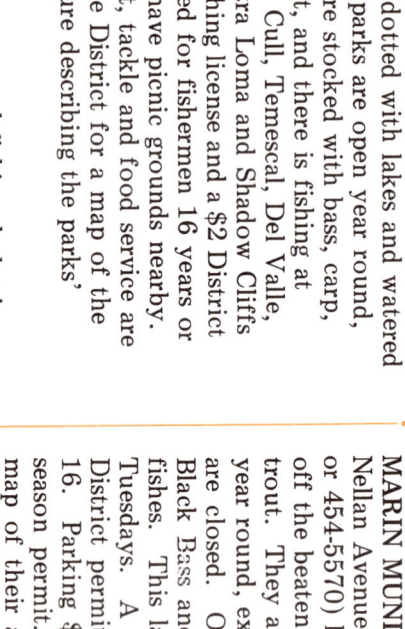

MARIN MUNICIPAL WATER DISTRICT (220 Nellan Avenue, Corte Madera 94925, 924-4600 or 454-5570) has a number of lakes, small and off the beaten paths, which are stocked with trout. They are open to the public for fishing year round, except for Tuesdays when the lakes are closed. One lake, Nicasio, is stocked with Black Bass and the warm water variety of fishes. This lake is open each day, including Tuesdays. A state fishing license and Water District permits are required for fishermen over 16. Parking $1 per car per day, or $5 for a season permit. Call or write the District for a map of their area showing the lakes.

POINT REYES NATIONAL SEASHORE (Point Reyes Station, 663-1092) affords good ocean fishing for a variety of fish from shore or from a boat. There is some freshwater fishing in several small ponds. A fishing license is required for all fishermen 16 years or older. For further information, contact the National Seashore.

Directions: Highway 101 north to Sir Francis Drake Boulevard, and west to Point Reyes.

HIKING. The San Francisco Bay chapter of the Sierra Club (5608 College Avenue, Oakland, 658-7470) encourages visitors to take part in its Bay Area outings. These vary from short, easy walks, through hikes with some climbing, to more demanding knapsack trips. Children of all ages are welcome if capable of participating. Hikes are conducted Saturday and Sunday by volunteer leaders and are a good way for young people to meet friends and become familiar with local recreation areas. A printed schedule of activities is available for 50 cents.

Directions: BART Rockridge Station, south on College Avenue. By car, Highway 580 to Highway 24, Claremont Avenue exit, east on Claremont to College and turn right.

LINCOLN PARK, in the northwest corner of San Francisco, has hiking and bicycle trails with views of the sea on north and west. Windy, but beautiful.

Directions: Lake Street to El Camino del Mar.

REDWOOD REGIONAL PARK (Skyline Boulevard and Redwood Road, Oakland, 531-9300) in the hills which border Oakland on the east, is a hiker's and rider's park. It is developed only with trails. A trail is being developed from Redwood to Tilden Park, 26 continuous miles, with camping sites for overnight backpackers. There are second growth redwoods here and a profusion of wild flowers in season.

Directions: Cross Bay Bridge, take MacArthur Freeway (Highway 580) to 35th Avenue exit, left on 35th which becomes Redwood Road, to park entrance.

23

MUIR WOODS (17 miles north of San Francisco) is a park for hiking — its six miles of trails join those of other public lands to the top of Mount Tamalpais or to the ocean. There are bridges over Redwood Creek, and trailside exhibits, signs and markers for guides. You will find park rangers on the trails and at the visitor center if you need information or help. Snacks and souvenirs are sold near the visitor center. No picnicking or camping sites are maintained, but you can picnic wherever you wish. No portable radios are permitted and pets must be kept on a leash. Redwoods over 200 feet tower over the trails which are bordered by fern and wildflowers.

Directions: Cross Golden Gate Bridge; take Highway 101 to Highway 1 to Panoramic Highway to Muir Woods Road.

BEAR VALLEY TRAILS (Point Reyes National Seashore, 663-1092) include the Woodpecker Trail, short and especially recommended for nature study; the Bear Valley Trail to the Divide Meadow (three miles round trip); and longer treks on the Sky Trail, Coast Trails, and fairly steep trails leading off the Bear Valley Trail. Camping allowed only with a permit and in designated campsites. No motorized vehicles allowed. The Ranger or Information Receptionist at the Bear Valley Ranger Station will supply you with a map of the area and answer your questions.

Directions: Cross Golden Gate Bridge, take Highway 1 to Olema, turn one mile west to Park Superintendent Headquarters on the Bear Valley Road. Trails start from here.

KITE FLYING. The Pacific Gas and Electric Company (S.F., 981-3232; East Bay, 834-1234; consult phone book for other areas) will send a lineman to remove any kite caught in electric wires, but has issued several safety warnings to kite-flyers: Do not fly kites near electric lines; avoid any use of metallic string, wire, or other metal parts in the construction or use of a kite; never use a wet string; and if the kite gets caught in a power line, leave it alone.

NATURE PROGRAMS. The Walnut Creek Department of Parks and Recreation has a lively museum called the Alexander Lindsay Junior Museum (1901 First Avenue, 935-1978) with tame, wild animals on exhibit, a pet library for children and adults, a traveling nature program for schools and community groups, a wildlife rescue and release program and many more activities. Open 1-5 Tuesday through Friday, 10-5 Saturday, closed Sunday and Monday.

Directions: Highway 580 to Highway 24 to Geary Road exit, turn south to 1st Ave.

LOUISE A. BOYD MARIN MUSEUM OF SCIENCE (76 Albert Park Lane, San Rafael 94901, 454-6961) sponsors naturalist walks for preschool age children and their parents on Friday and Saturday mornings, led by Mrs. Elizabeth Terwilleger of Mill Valley. The walks (those on Saturday were planned so fathers could go along too) are from 9:30 am to 12:30 pm. They are geared to preschoolers. The destination is one of the nature preserves and birds, plants, trees and small animals are identified along the way. The walks end in a picnic lunch — everyone brings his own. There is a fee to the museum of $10 for members, $13 for nonmembers for a Friday or Saturday series of six weeks. Registration is for the series only.

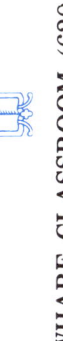

OLD WHARF CLASSROOM (620-A Central Avenue, Alameda, 524-1034) conducts a number of programs led by staff naturalists on marine ecology, bay and ocean currents, whales, fish, insects, and similar subjects during the months of May and June. The programs are on Sunday afternoons and are free. There's sandy beach, swimming and picnicking nearby.

Directions: BART Fruitvale Station and AC 63 or 64 bus. By car, Highway 17 south to Jackson Street, through the Webster Street tube to stop light at Central Avenue. Turn right on Central for ½ block, then left on McKay. Last building on left hand side of street.

EAST BAY REGIONAL PARKS – A unique experience is offered by the nature staff of some of the East Bay parks. Park naturalists conduct walks to look for or listen to woodland creatures and explore an oak forest. There's the indian shell mound where visitors travel 3,000 years into the past to learn where and how the first Californians lived, or a walk to search out and investigate the plants used by California's first inhabitants for survival, or an exploration of the hills and meadows during wildflower season (the month of May). There's also a walk to trace the history of a park valley beginning with the first American homesteaders, following the path of their arrival, with stops at historic sites along the way. Naturalist hikes start the end of February and continue through September. Phone for a month-by-month schedule. Coyote Hills (Newark) 471-4967; Sunol Park, 862-2244; Tilden/Alameda Beach, 524-1034.

LAKE CHABOT (Anthony Chabot Regional Park, San Leandro, 531-9300) has a free boat tour on Sundays in August from 12 noon to 2:30 pm. Families explore the watery realm of Lake Chabot with a naturalist and discover the forms of life that dwell there. Children have a chance to assist the naturalist in using scientific tools to test the temperature and water clarity. Advance registration required. Fee 75 cents per person. Phone for registration. After the boat trip, stay on for the free late Sunday Afternoon Programs, 4 to 5:30 pm at the Lake Chabot Picnic Area, when a naturalist discusses snakes, plants, birds, or bugs and creepy crawlers. Parking, 50 cents.

Directions: Cross Bay Bridge; take MacArthur Freeway to Dutton Avenue off-ramp, then Estudillo Avenue to Lake Chabot Drive.

BIO-SONAR LABORATORY (Coyote Hills Regional Park, 8000 Patterson Ranch Road, Fremont, 531-9300) arranges free guided tours to meet seals, sea lions and otters and examine equipment used to study their ability to "see without using their eyes." Sandy the Sea Lion is a favorite performer. Tours are conducted during the spring on the first Saturday of each month from noon until 4 pm, with sea lion performances at 1 and 3:30 pm. Parking at picnic area. The park also contains ancient Indian shell mounds and is a wildlife refuge.

Directions: Nimitz Freeway or Dumbarton Bridge to Jarvis Street to Newark Boulevard. Right on Newark to Patterson Ranch Road.

SUNOL VALLEY REGIONAL PARK (Sunol, 862-2244) conducts nature studies on Sunday afternoons in August. A naturalist may explore the watery world of Alameda Creek, for instance, lecturing on food webs and catching and examining the strange creatures which live their lives unseen beneath the algae. Bathing suits and tennis shoes recommended. Free.

Directions: Cross Bay Bridge; take Highway 580 to Highway 680, then south to Calaveras Road. Follow Calaveras south to Geary Road and left to park entrance.

PICNICKING. Most of the parks in San Francisco have picnic areas. There are sites in Fleishhacker, Julius Kahn, McLaren, Mountain Lake, Stern Grove, Glen Park Canyon and Golden Gate. There are no *Keep Off the Grass* signs and you can picnic where you please. In Golden Gate Park there's the added attraction of a children's playground, on South Drive near Kezar Stadium, with slides, swings, a San Francisco cable car, a small farmyard with pigs, goats, rabbits and chickens, and a merry-go-round. A snack bar is open until 5 pm. Park maps and brochures are available free from the Park Department, 558-4268.

LAKESIDE PARK (between Grand and Lakeshore Avenues, Oakland, 273-3296) boasts a lake, Japanese garden, wild life refuge, and, from mid-June until October, Sunday concerts at 2:30 pm for post-picnic relaxation. Or take the little park bus, the Lakeside Lark, to additional picnic areas in Children's Fairyland.

Directions: BART 19th Street Station. By car, Highway 580 to the Grand Avenue off ramp, turn right.

EAST BAY REGIONAL PARK DISTRICT (11500 Skyline Boulevard, Oakland, 531-9300). The 27 magnificent parks in the East Bay have extensive picnic grounds and recreational facilities, many with food service. Parks are open every day, 8 am to 10 pm. Some have parking fees: Temescal, 75 cents; Lake Anza area in Tilden, Roberts and Chabot, 50 cents; Kennedy Grove, 25 cents. For a detailed map showing location of parks and a description of additional attractions such as golf, boating, horse trails, swimming, contact the EBRPD.

ANGEL ISLAND STATE PARK (off Tiburon, Marin County, 435-9111) is reached by ferry and is a great spot for picnicking, bicycling and hiking. Ayala Cove (ferry landing) has picnic sites, with charcoal for sale, and there are also tables, barbecue stoves and comfort stations at West Garrison. No cars are allowed on the island.

The island is a federal and state wilclife refuge for deer, birds, and waterfowl and contains varied and exotic flowers from all over the world. At present the ferry from San Francisco to Angel Island will not carry bicycles, but this policy may change somewhere along the line, so you might check again (398-1141). However, the ferry from Tiburon to Angel Island does allow you to bring your bike at no extra cost. There are several miles of hard-surfaced, hilly roads on the island and 12 miles of marked hiking trails, two of which reach the summit of the 776-foot Mt. Caroline Livermore. Other activities include fishing and sunbathing (no swimming) at Ayala Cove. Visitors to Angel Island also get a spectacular 360-degree panoramic view of the entire Bay Area, including the Golden Gate, Bay, and Richmond bridges; Alcatraz, Treasure and Yerba Buena islands; the skyline of San Francisco and Oakland; and the mountains of the East Bay and Marin.

Admission to park, 25 cents; children under 12, free. Open 8 am to sunset, all year round.

MT. TAMALPAIS STATE PARK (801

Panoramic Highway, Mill Valley) is one of the most popular areas for picnicking, hiking and camping. On a clear day you can see almost forever from the top of Mt. Tam (altitude 2,604) which can be reached on a winding road by car. Wildflowers abound in the spring.

Directions: Cross Golden Gate Bridge and take Highway 101 to Highway 1 to Panoramic Highway.

BAY MEADOWS RACE COURSE (between El Camino Real and Bayshore Freeway, at Hillsdale Boulevard, San Mateo, 345-1661) holds workouts every Saturday from 8 to 9 am from early September to late December, with training races starting at 9:15. From 9 to 10:45 am there is a tour of the barns and a film on racing. Snack bar. Admission free.

Directions: Bayshore Freeway south to Hillsdale Boulevard off-ramp.

GOLDEN GATE FIELDS RACE COURSE (1100 Eastshore Highway, Albany, 526-3020) holds workouts open to the public daily during Easter Week, and Saturdays only thereafter to mid-June from 8 to 10:30 am. Tour of stables and a racing film are added attractions. Admission free.

Directions: BART North Berkeley Station and AC 94 bus during horse-racing season only. By car, Highway 80 north to Albany turnoff.

ROCK CLIMBING. Beginners can learn climbing techniques under the supervision of experienced Sierra Club climbers at all of these sites. It is not necessary to be a Sierra Club member to participate in these instruction sessions. For age limitations and other information, call the Bay Chapter office, 658-7470.

MIRALOMA in San Francisco (Portola Drive to O'Shaughnessy Boulevard to Glen Park Playground, then follow the canyon 1/4 mile to climbing site); **GRIZZLY CAVES** in Berkeley (Grizzly Peak Boulevard, 1/2 mile northwest of Miniature Railroad, Tilden Park); **PINNACLE ROCK** in Berkeley (Remillard Park, Keeler Avenue and Poppy Lane); and rocks near the summit of **MT. TAMALPAIS** in Marin County (Golden Gate Bridge to Panoramic Drive in Mill Valley) are all fun to clamber over.

SAILBOAT RENTALS — Sailboats can be rented by the hour, day, week or month from the John Beery Sailing School, Berkeley (Aquatic Park, 845-6310; Alameda Marina (1815 Clement, 623-8500); and Sausalito (2650 Bridgeway, 332-5138). Hourly rates run from $2 to $5 per hour depending on the boat, with special weekly and monthly rates.

LAKE MERRITT SAILBOAT HOUSE (568 Bellevue Avenue, Oakland, 444-3807) has sailboats for rent. Regattas in spring, summer and fall.

Directions: BART 19th Street Station. By car, Highway 580 to exit at Grand Avenue, turn right to Bellevue Avenue, and left to the boathouse.

THE CALIFORNIA STATE AUTOMOBILE ASSOCIATION maintains a telephone information service (ski phone, 864-6440) on weather and skiing conditions. It operates 24 hours a day, all week.

THE CALIFORNIA DIVISION OF HIGHWAYS also maintains recorded and up-to-date 24-hour phone reports on highway conditions (557-3755).

NATIONAL PARK SERVICE, U.S. Department of the Interior (556-4122) offers facilities in several parks for downhill and cross-country skiing, snowmobiling, and other winter sports. The parks put their emphasis on cross-country skiing — something that cannot be done to a great extent at commercial ski developments, and which children and parents can enjoy together.

LASSEN VOLCANIC NATIONAL PARK

(Mineral 96063, 916-595-2711) has its winter season from mid-December through early April. Lassen Peak, last active in 1921, is the focal point of this 106,000-acre national park of hot springs, steam and gas vents (fumaroles). At Sulphur Works entrance station there is an 1100-foot Poma lift, 400-foot rope tow, 200-foot rope tow for beginners, a ski school, a ski shop with rentals, a ski school, and ski patrol. Open 10 am to 4 pm, Saturdays, Sundays, and holidays only; supervised by park rangers. There are four marked trails for cross-country skiers. One 3/4-mile route leads to Sulphur Works hot springs with its boiling mud pots. There is snowmobiling, tobogganing on tubes and platters, and camping (no designated areas, bring your own tent). There is a cafeteria, lounge, parking area and first aid station, but no overnight accommodations in the park. These can be obtained in nearby Mineral (916-595-4444).

Directions: Take Highway 80 over the Bay Bridge and drive north to Interstate 5. Take Interstate 5 to Red Bluff, then right on Highway 36 to Lassen.

STAR GAZING

Twilight star parties are a feature at both Del Valle Regional Park, Livermore, and Sunol Valley Regional Park, Sunol. Park naturalists conduct meetings Saturday at dusk once a month, April through October, with viewings through telescopes and lectures on constellations, planets and other celestial objects. Bring a warm jacket and your own binoculars or telescope if you wish. For dates and park locations, phone East Bay Regional Park District Interpretive Department, 531-9300.

Directions: Highway 580 for both. For Del

Valle, get off at Portola Road, Livermore, to South Livermore Avenue, to Tesla Road, to Mines Road. For Sunol Park, turn off at Highway 680, then take Calaveras Road to Geary Road.

SANTA CRUZ BEACH, 84 miles south of San Francisco, is the closest beach for surfing. It's worth the trip because the beach is spacious and the surfing excellent. There's also a boardwalk, amusement park and pier for fishing, shopping and eating seafood.

Directions: Highway 101 south to Highway 17; then west to Santa Cruz. Or take the scenic, but slower, Highway 1 south.

ANTHONY CHABOT REGIONAL PARK (Oakland-San Leandro, 531-9300) offers a marksmanship range for rifle, pistol and trap shooting.

Directions: MacArthur Freeway to 35th Avenue turnoff (East Oakland). Left on 35th toward hills, becomes Redwood Road.

Continue past intersection of Skyline, 6.3 miles, to Marciel Gate entrance to park.

BRIONES REGIONAL PARK (between Orinda, Lafayette, Pleasant Hill and Martinez, 531-9043) is a semi-wilderness area of over 3,000 acres, ideal for hiking, picnicking and horseback riding (stables near park) through its rolling hills, wooded sunny ravines and valleys. A unique feature of Briones is that no cars are allowed; they must park in a small entrance area where there are picnic grounds and a children's playpark. The rest of the park is kept in its natural state. A wildflower kit with illustrations and historical background of flowers in the area is available. Two shelters for youth group camping (by reservation only, 531-9043).

Directions: Cross Bay Bridge, take Highway 80 north to San Pablo Dam Road to Bear Creek Road.

SEAL ROCKS lie about 400 feet offshore at the northern end of Ocean Beach, on Great Highway. Here, not seals, but sea lions bask in the sun or play in the water, some so big they are said to weigh more than a ton. Seal Rocks is also the best place in early spring to watch the grey whales on their annual migration north from their breeding grounds in Baja California to summer in the Bering Sea.

Directions: Take Van Ness Avenue north to Geary Boulevard and follow Geary west to the ocean.

AMERICAN RIVER TOURING ASSN., INC. (1016 Jackson Street, Oakland, 465-9355) conducts white water raft trips in the gold rush country every weekend spring, summer and fall. A discount is offered children 12 and under, as well as to young adults 13 to 17. This group conducts many of the Sierra Club's trips down various rivers.

Directions: Cross the Bay Bridge, take the Nimitz Freeway to the Jackson Street off-ramp.

AUDUBON CANYON RANCH (Bolinas Lagoon, Marin County, 383-1644) is a sanctuary for the common egret and the blue heron. Each spring the great birds come from as far south as Baja California to nest high in the redwood trees. Bolinas Lagoon, a county wildlife refuge, serves as feeding ground for the nesting herons and egrets as well as for 55 species of waterfowl and 90 species of migrant shorebirds. The peak of the nesting season is from March through July 4, during which time the ranch is open to the public from 10 am to 4 pm, Saturday, Sunday, and holidays.

A self-guiding trail behind the ranchhouse leads up the canyon to Henderson Overlook where there are benches and a telescope trained on one of the nests in the trees. There are easy hiking trails around the area which is ablaze with wild flowers in spring. A naturalist is at the information office to answer questions and explain the habits of the birds. No pets allowed. Free.

Directions: Cross Golden Gate Bridge and take Highway 1 to Bolinas Lagoon.

Children's Concerts, Films, TV & Theater

SAN FRANCISCO SYMPHONY ORCHESTRA (107 War Memorial Veterans' Building, Civic Center, S.F., 861-6240) performs a series of four concerts each spring for grades 4 to 8, presented in the Opera House and at concert facilities in surrounding Bay Area communities. Talented student musicians appear from time to time as inspiring guest soloists before audiences of their peers. Parents may attend with students. Admission $1.25.

UNIVERSITY OF CALIFORNIA, MUSIC DEPARTMENT (Berkeley, 642-2678) presents a free 45-minute concert every Wednesday at 12:15 pm during the school year. Performances take place at Hertz Memorial Hall, on campus, near College and Bancroft. Compositions by graduate students, traditional music, and occasional jazz are performed. The concerts are open to the public. Pre-school youngsters cannot be admitted. School groups should call 642-4864 in advance.

Directions: BART Berkeley station and AC 40, 51 or 58 bus. By car, Highway 80 north to University Avenue exit, right to Oxford Street, right to Durant Street, left to College Avenue and left again to Bancroft Way.

JUNIOR BACH FESTIVAL (P.O. Box 590, Berkeley 94701, 845-4300) each spring offers four all Bach concerts for young people. The musicians, all 19 years old or under, are chosen at an annual audition (see details under Miscellany). The four matinee and evening concerts are held at Hertz Hall, University of California Berkeley, the end of April.

THE PALACE OF THE LEGION OF HONOR (Lincoln Park, S.F., 558-2881) has free organ recitals every Saturday and Sunday at 4 pm, year round. It also sponsors eight subscription are picnic tables and any of the lawn areas may be used for informal picnicking.

Directions: Take Fulton Street which begins one block west of City Hall to Park Presidio Boulevard, turn left through Golden Gate Park. On the other side of the Park you are on 19th Avenue. Follow this south to Sloat Boulevard.

GOLDEN GATE PARK MUSIC CONCOURSE (between California Academy of Sciences and the De Young Museum, off South Drive, 558-4277) is a shady glade where free concerts are held at 2 pm Sundays, year round, weather permitting. Special concerts are held at other times and other places, including Soul and Blues festivals and "Big Band" and Dixieland concerts in summer and fall. Watch newspapers or phone for schedules.

Directions; Take Fulton Street, one block west of City Hall, to Stanyon Street, turn left to Waller and into Golden Gate Park to South Drive.

concerts by nationally known artists during fall and winter. Subscription to series, from $12 for members to $18 for non-members; single admissions, members $3.50, non-members $4. Phone box office, 221-1232, for schedules and tickets.

Directions: Take Van Ness Avenue north to Geary Boulevard, turn right at 34th Avenue into Lincoln Park. 34th Avenue becomes Legion of Honor Drive to the museum.

STERN GROVE FESTIVAL ASSOCIATION (P.O. Box 3250, S.F. 94119, 398-6551 or 558-4728) sponsors free outdoor symphony concerts, operas, operettas, and ballets, Sunday afternoon, 2 pm, from mid-June to late August in Stern Grove, corner of 19th Avenue and Sloat Boulevard, S.F. The grove is a natural amphitheatre, a grass-carpeted glade sheltered by eucalyptus trees. There

OAKLAND SYMPHONY ASSOCIATION YOUTH CONCERTS (Latham Square Building, Oakland, 444-3531) sponsors two concerts for young people every year with the Oakland Public Schools at the Oakland Auditorium, corner of Oak at 10 Tenth Street. These are generally a symphony concert in the fall and an opera in the spring and five performances of each are given. Youth from Oakland and other cooperating schools are usually bussed to the auditorium. The concerts are open to all young people, if tickets are available. Series price $2 for Oaklanders and $3 for out-of-towners. Single concerts, if available, $1.50 at the door. Contact Music Department, Oakland Public Schools, 836-2622 for tickets.

Directions: BART 12th Street station. By car, Highway 17 to Oak Street exit, turn left under freeway to Tenth Street.

OAKLAND MUNICIPAL BAND (Oakland Department of Parks and Recreation, Burton Weber, 1520 Lakeside Drive, Oakland, 273-3062) gives outdoor concerts from June to early September every Sunday and the 4th of July at 2:30 pm at Lakeside Park, West Grand Avenue, Oakland. Fred Rose conducts the spirited 40-piece professional band. Free.

Directions: BART 19th Street station. By car, Highway 580 to the Grand Avenue exit. Turn right to Lakeside Drive.

SAN FRANCISCO MAIN PUBLIC LIBRARY (Civic Center, Children's Room, 558-3510) shows free movies for kids 6 years old and upwards the first and third Tuesday of every month at 4 pm. The films are both animated cartoons and live performances based on children's storybooks. The programs last one hour.

Directions: This is across the Plaza from City Hall on Larkin and McAllister Streets.

THE SAN FRANCISCO MUSEUM OF ART (4th Floor, War Memorial Veterans' Building, Van Ness and McAllister Street, S.F., 863-8800) shows films for children one Saturday a month in the auditorium. These films are suitable for children aged 6 to 12 and are generally shown the second or third Saturday of each month at 1 pm. Phone for exact information. Free.

Directions: Across the street from City Hall.

ELECTROVISION THEATRE (Bing Crosby's San Francisco Experience, atop Ghirardelli Square, 3rd Floor of Old Mustard Building, S.F.) uses 30 specially computerized projectors simultaneously propelling thousands of separate pictures on a giant screen curving nearly 180 degrees, with sound and color. The 200-year history of San Francisco is portrayed including the earthquake and fire of 1906. The stereo sounds of foghorns, bells and staccato noises of San Francisco probably makes this cinematic entertainment too exciting for the younger set, but it should be of interest to older kids. Electrovision was first shown at Expo 67, Montreal, and Expo 70, Osaka. Adults, $1.75; children under 12, $1. Continuous performances daily from 11:15 am.

Directions: Van Ness north to Northpoint Street, turn right two blocks.

THE LAWRENCE HALL OF SCIENCE

(University of California Berkeley, 642-5132) offers a fascinating series of scientific films and lectures oriented to children. Films are shown Saturday and Sunday at 11 am, 1 pm and 3:45 pm. Evening showings at 7:30 pm Thursday, Friday and Saturday. Films have included topics such as mountain climbing, animal behavior and photography. Lecture-demonstrations are presented Saturday and Sunday at 2:30 pm. Films are included in admission fee: adults, $1, students, 50 cents, children 12 and under, 25 cents, under 6 free. Group rate 25 cents per person.

Directions: BART Berkeley station and AC 51 bus, but it's a long walk uphill. By car, Highway 80 north to University Avenue exit, turn right to Oxford, left to Hearst Avenue, then right to Gayley Avenue, left on Gayley to Rimway Road, left to Centennial Drive, and left again to top of the hill.

UNIVERSITY ART MUSEUM

(2626 Bancroft Way, Berkeley, 642-1412) shows art, dance and foreign films Tuesdays through Sundays, 7:30 to 9:30 pm. Tickets are 75 cents. Entrance on Durant Street. Phone for program.

Directions: BART Berkeley station and AC 40, 51 or 58 bus. By car, Highway 80 north to University off-ramp. Follow this to Oxford Street, turn right to Durant Street and left to Bowditch Street. One block beyond is College Street and the movie entrance is between the two streets.

THE OAKLAND MUSEUM (1000 Oak Street, Oakland 273-3401) often features film series, revivals, etc., in the museum's 300-seat theater. Phone ahead for schedule and admission charge.

Directions: BART Lake Merritt station. By car, Highway 17 to Oak Street off-ramp, turn left under freeway to 10th Street.

COLLEGE OF ALAMEDA (Community Services, 522-7221) offers a free film series every Tuesday evening at 7 in the Little Theater, Alameda High School, 2200 Central Avenue, Alameda. The films include classic productions suitable mainly for older children. Call first for program.

Directions: BART 12th Street station and AC 51 or 58 bus. By car, Highway 17 to the Park Street off-ramp. Turn right to Central Avenue.

THE SAN FRANCISCO CHILDREN'S OPERA (245 - 10th Avenue, S.F., 386-9622) gives six or more opera performances between September and May each year at the Roosevelt Junior High School Auditorium (480 Arguello Boulevard, near Geary Boulevard). Among the operas performed are *Little Red Riding Hood*, *The Emperor's New Clothes* and *Sinbad the Sailor*. This unique program is the only children's opera company in the United States. Children are selected through auditions by Dr. Norbert Gingold, director. Reservations should be made early for any performance, since they are usually sold out well in advance. Admission is $2, $2.50 and $3. Phone for applications or reservations.

Directions: Take Van Ness Avenue north to Geary Boulevard, turn left to 10th Avenue, then right.

SAN FRANCISCO RECREATIONAL ARTS BUILDING (50 Scott Street, S.F., 588-4089) sponsors several year round puppet shows for small children. Performances are given by various local artists. The performances are scheduled at various city playgrounds on Saturdays during the winter and also on weekdays during summer vacation. All programs are free. Phone for more exact information on dates and places.

MILL VALLEY PUPPETEERS (Ruth Callahan, 383-0143) is the professional name of the Wentworth Family which, with its 75 puppets, puts on performances in the Bay Area. Once a year, in the spring, they put on three shows in one day in Mill Valley. The Wentworths specialize in telling folk tales from different lands and cultures. Examples of their shows are *How the Bears Came Into the Land* (Russian) and *How the Elephant Got His Trunk* (from Kipling). Sounds and music representative of the different countries are included. Phone for schedule. The Wentworths also perform for clubs, schools and birthday parties.

CHILDREN'S THEATRE ASSOCIATION OF SAN FRANCISCO (821 Market Street, San Francisco) is a nonprofit agency that puts on four or five plays a year for ages 3 to 10. The plays are generally fairy tales, with marionette or live performers. Performances are scheduled between September and March each year, on Saturday mornings and afternoons, at different public school auditoriums. Tickets 50 cents. Phone for schedule and dates.

THE NEW SHAKESPEARE COMPANY (1668 Bush Street, S.F., 771-5290) is a professional group which performs during the winter throughout the United States and Canada at colleges and high schools, under the guidance of director Margrit Roma and producer Clarence Rickleff. Each summer they stage afternoon outdoor productions such as *A Midsummer Night's Dream* and *As You Like It*, in Golden Gate Park. Performances take place Saturdays and Sundays at 2 pm over a period of three to five weeks. Admission is free, but donations are appreciated. Phone for performance dates.

PYRAMUS AND THISBE CHILDREN'S THEATRE (Live Oak Recreation Center, Shattuck Avenue and Berryman, Berkeley, 845-1718) stages musicals, fairy tales, science fiction, and audience participation performances for children of all ages, every Saturday at 10 am. Group's work has been widely acclaimed and highly successful. For program call Center or Director Thomas Lynch, 843-9175.

Directions: BART Berkeley Station and AC F or 67 bus. By car, Highway 80 north to University Avenue exit, turn right to Shattuck and left to Berryman.

CHANNEL 9, KQED (525 4th Street, S.F., 864-2000) invites audiences to an occasional special program. Listen to programs for announcements or phone Programming Dept.

BAY AREA RAPID TRANSIT

Routes	Monday-Saturday	Nights and Sunday
Concord-Daly City	through service	through service
Richmond-Daly City	through service	transfer at MacArthur
Richmond-Fremont	through service	through service
Fremont-Daly City	transfer at MacArthur	transfer at MacArthur
Richmond-Concord	transfer at MacArthur	transfer at MacArthur
Concord-Fremont	transfer at 12th St.-Oakland	transfer at 12th St.-Oakland

Embarcadero
Montgomery St
Powell St
Civic Center

Glen Park
Balboa Park
Daly City

16th St Mission
24th St Mission

Oakland West

MacArthur
19th St Oakland
Oakland City Center -12th St

Lake Merritt

Fruitvale
Coliseum
San Leandro
Bay Fair
Hayward
South Hayward
Union City
Fremont

Richmond
El Cerrito Del Norte
El Cerrito Plaza
North Berkeley
Berkeley
Ashby

Orinda
Rockridge

Lafayette
Walnut Creek
Pleasant Hill
Concord

N →

FREE TOURS

AIRPORT NATIONAL WEATHER SERVICE (S.F. International Airport, Central Terminal, Room 507, South S.F., 876-9500) schedules half-hour tours for fifth graders and up any day the office is not too busy. Kids are shown office operations, equipment and duties of the personnel, and how the weather is recorded locally, nationally and worldwide. By appointment only. Tours for groups of 20 which families may arrange to join.

Directions: Bayshore Freeway south to Airport turnoff.

AIRPORTS COMMISSION (S.F. International Airport, 94128; Public Relations 876-2222 or 761-0800) conducts 1½-hour tours Tuesday through Saturday at 10 am and 1 pm, year round, holidays excepted. Kids visit terminal shops, ticket counters, luggage claiming areas and spectators' deck to watch jetliners land and take off. It is usually possible to board and walk through a jetliner. Tours are only by groups of 5 to 10, supervised by an adult. Write or telephone for an application form 15 days in advance.

Directions: Bayshore Freeway (US 101) south to Airport Terminals exit.

SF-O HELIPORT (Oakland International Airport, Earhart Road, Hangar 9, Oakland, 635-2222, Mr. Klement or Mr. Stoffers) flies helicopters between San Francisco, Berkeley, Sausalito, and Oakland. Kids are shown the maintenance facilities where helicopters are repaired, how a helicopter functions, and can sometimes board one to see where the pilot sits and the passengers ride. Tour appointments must be made in advance, and only groups of 10 or more are acceptable. Individuals may call to see if they can join the next tour.

Directions: BART Coliseum station and AC 57 C bus. By car, Highway 17 south to Airport exit.

OAKLAND INTERNATIONAL AIRPORT (Doolittle Drive and Airport Drive, Oakland, 462-4165, Mrs. Ziegler) conducts children through the main terminal Monday through Sunday year round on 30-minute tours. Kids visit the observation deck, ticket counter, and watch luggage being processed. Tours are every half hour from 10 am to 3 pm, for age groups from third grade and up, with a minimum of 12 and a maximum of 30 persons. Individuals can call to see if they can join an upcoming group. It may also be possible to visit a PSA jetliner, if circumstances permit, on the same day as your tour. Call PSA Tour Service, 836-4043, for information.

Directions: BART Coliseum station and AC 57 C bus. By car, Highway 17 south to Airport exit.

STRYBING ARBORETUM (South Drive, adjacent to Ninth Avenue and Lincoln Way, Golden Gate Park, S.F., 661-0822) has guided tours at 11 am and 2 pm, Thursdays and Saturdays, February through November. The Arboretum contains 70 acres of more than 5,000 rare and exotic plants from the Himalayas to Tierra del Fuego. Open Monday through Friday, 8:30 am to 4:30 pm, weekends and holidays from 10 am to 5 pm. No reservations needed for family groups. There is an unusual "Garden of Fragrance," with plant labels in Braille, demonstration gardens and various nature walks. Tours start from arboretum entrance, located next to Hall of Flowers.

Directions: Fell Street west to Stanyan Street, turn left to Lincoln Way, then right to 9th Avenue.

KILPATRICK'S BAKERIES, INC. (2030 Folsom Street, S.F., 431-0810, Mrs. Kuenzel) conducts 45-minute tours for second graders and up. Kids can see ingredients made into dough, the fermentation process, loaves formed and put into ovens, and finished bread sliced and wrapped. Guides orient their talks to the age group on tour so that children learn while they watch. At the end, each child gets a hot dog bun, a pencil, and a booklet describing the breadbaking process. By appointment only.

Directions: Van Ness Avenue south, turn left at 16th Street, then right on Folsom Street.

MOTHER'S COOKIES (810 - 81st Avenue, Oakland, 569-2323, Mrs. Soffiotto) offers tours of the plant on Tuesdays and Thursdays at 9 am and 11 am, maximum group size 30, and minimum five or six. Minimum age level is 6 years old, and there should be one adult for each six children. Kids are shown how cookies are mixed, shaped, baked, packaged, warehoused and shipped. They are given a bag of cookies at the end of the tour and a leaflet explaining the process they have just seen. This is a popular tour and reservations must be made as much as three or four months in advance.

Directions: BART Coliseum station. By car, Highway 17 to 66th Avenue turnoff, turn right at San Leandro Street, then left at 81st Avenue.

NESTLE COMPANY (900 East Blanco Road, Salinas 93901, 408-424-2571) will take visitors on a tour of its chocolate factory on Tuesdays and Fridays at 9:30 and 10:15 am. Demonstrations of how candy and chocolate syrup are made, from the chocolate bean to the finished candy bar. There is also a half-hour film of the history of candy and chocolate manufacture. Free admission and free samples. Reservations advised.

Directions: Highway 101 south to Sanborn Road exit, west on Sanborn, which becomes Blanco Road.

CABLE CAR BARN (Washington and Mason Streets, 558-3382, Mr. Cann) is open from 10 am to 10 pm on Friday, Saturday and Sunday and 10 am to 6 pm on Monday through Thursday year round. Reservations for a group tour should be made about a week in advance, but a family may join such a tour at any time. The tour includes a lecture on the history and mechanics of the cable car, a visit to the repair shops, the "roost" for cars not in use, with a question and answer period at the end. Kids can watch cable car machinery in operation, see (on a model) how the cars are pulled along at 9 miles an hour when the gripman (or conductor) pulls a lever which closes a pincer grip on the cable. One of inventor Hallidie's first cable cars, over 100 years old, is downstairs in the museum.

Directions: Van Ness Avenue north to Washington Street, turn right seven blocks. Or better yet, take cable car at Powell and Market, Beach and Hyde, Bay and Taylor as they all pass by the Cable Car Museum at 1201 Mason.

ST. MARY'S CATHEDRAL (Geary and Gough Streets, S.F.) is one of San Francisco's newest tourist attractions. Its architectural interest is its radical departure from the traditional cruciform structure. No pillars obstruct the congregation's view of the altar and the great soaring cupola, intersected by stained glass windows that form a cross at the top, is supported along its edges by vaults and pylons, a marvel of engineering. A walk around the outside of the cathedral affords the visitor a good view of the city. Good for would-be architects and budding builders.

Directions: Take Van Ness Avenue north to Geary Boulevard, turn left two blocks to Gough Street.

MORMON TEMPLE (The Church of Jesus Christ of Latter-day Saints, 4780 Lincoln Avenue, 531-1475, Oakland) welcomes visitors to the grounds under the direction of a guide (only qualified Mormons are admitted to the temple). The temple stands on a hill, overlooking San Francisco Bay. During the day, it can be seen from as far away as the Golden Gate and at night, illuminated, it can be seen for many miles. In the foreground are fountains and a cascade of water, and the visitor has a panoramic view of the entire Bay area.

Visiting hours, May-October, Monday through Saturday, 9 am to 9 pm, Sunday 10 am to 9 pm.

Directions: BART 12th Street station and AC 15A bus. By car, Highway 580 to Fruitvale turnoff, left on Fruitvale Avenue to MacArthur Boulevard to Lincoln Avenue.

LEVI STRAUSS & CO. (250 Valencia Street, S.F., 391-6200) offers free tours of the factory where world-renowned blue jeans are made, Tuesday through Thursday at 10:30 am, by appointment only.

Directions: Van Ness Avenue south to Market Street, turn right to Valencia, then left.

SAN FRANCISCO FIRE DEPARTMENT (26(Golden Gate Avenue, 861-8000, Office of the Chief) will take 13-year-olds and up on a tour of a firehouse. Arrangements must be made in advance for a fire station that is not having a drill, or otherwise busy.

The fire boats are docked at Pier 22½ on the Embarcadero, south of the Ferry Building opposite Harrison Street. The firemen at the station will be glad to explain from the pier how the boat functions, but it cannot be boarded. Make arrangements in advance.

Directions: Fire Department Headquarters is one block east of the Civic Center. Pier 22½ is four blocks south of Market Street on the Embarcadero. Take Van Ness Avenue south to Mission Street, turn left to the Embarcadero and right to Pier 22½.

OAKLAND FIRE DEPT. AND FIREHOUSE (1330 Grove Street, Oakland, 444-9625) and **OAKLAND FIREBOAT** (29 Jack London Square, Oakland, 832-4592) will take kids on a tour of a firehouse and even let them board a harbor fireboat if it is not in use and no drill is taking place. Ask for officer on duty. Tours are conducted year round, take about half an hour and are scheduled between 1 and 4 pm. Maximum group is 10; minimum age is 10 years old. At the firehouse kids are shown fire engine, hose wagon and pumper and told how they respond to the gong alarm system when reports of fire are phoned in and relayed to the firehouses. The tour of a fireboat includes the history and function of this form of fire fighting. Plan to call for an appointment a few days in advance.

Directions: Firehouse, BART 12th Street station. By car, Highway 17 to Market Street exit (becomes 5th Street) to Grove Street. Left to 13th Street. Fireboat, BART 12th Street station and AC 11, 33, 34, 59, or 76 bus. By car, Highway 17 to Market Street exit (becomes 5th Street) to Broadway. Right to Jack London Square.

BERKELEY FIRE DEPARTMENT (2029 Berkeley Way, 845-8500) welcomes visits to its fire stations by individuals or small groups. There is no minimum age limit but children should be accompanied by an adult. There are seven firehouses and a visit may be arranged, by appointment, to whichever one is most convenient. Includes explanation of equipment and apparatus, the handling of primary and secondary alarms, and the system of bells that alerts everybody in the house.

Directions: BART Berkeley Station, walk north. By car, Highway 80 north to University off-ramp, right to Shattuck and turn left one block to Berkeley Way.

GERBER PRODUCTS CO. (9401 San Leandro Street, Oakland, 569-1100, Mrs. De Costa) will schedule family tours or groups of up to 20 kids Monday, Wednesday and Friday from 10 am to 3 pm, ages 7 and up. The tours take 30 to 45 minutes and demonstrate the manufacture of baby foods from raw materials through preparation, cooking, bottling and boxing for shipping. Call in advance for an appointment.

Directions: Highway 17 or 580 to 98th Avenue exit. Proceed to the Gerber plant at 801-98th Avenue.

FOREMOST FOODS, CO. (366 Guerrero Street, S.F. 94103, 431-6000, Miss Rangel) takes second graders and up on a 30-minute tour of its ice-cream making plant. Children can see the cream being prepared, how the tremendous freezers run and the final frozen product, which can also be sampled, as distribution of Van Dandy Bars makes a happy ending to the tour. Group tours by appointment only. Individuals may join scheduled group tours, so call for openings.

Directions: Take Van Ness Avenue south to Market Street. Turn right to Guerrero, then left.

BERKELEY FARMS (4550 San Pablo Avenue, Emeryville, 652-9924) has tours of its dairy by appointment Tuesday through Thursday, showing processing and bottling of milk.

Directions: BART MacArthur station and AC 57 bus. By car, Highway 580 to San Pablo Avenue exit, turn north.

STANDARD OIL COMPANY OF CALIFORNIA (555 Market Street, S.F., 894-4895) has a permanent exhibit, "World of Oil," that shows how oil is found, produced, refined and marketed, through working models, moving displays and motion picture, actual oil field equipment, and three historical dioramas. Open 9:30 am to 4 pm, Monday through Friday. Group tours may be arranged by calling 894-4895.

Directions: Take Golden Gate Avenue east to Market Street, turn left to 555.

SAN FRANCISCO POLICE DEPARTMENT (850 Bryant Street, 94103) conducts two separate 1½-hour tours, Monday through Friday, one for senior high school age and over (Community Relations, 553-1231) and one for fourth graders through junior high school (School Safety Detail, 553-1617). Groups should not exceed 20. Families may call to join a group already set up. The tours include a visit to the crime lab, ID Bureau,

53

record room, juvenile bureau, photo lab, police and line-up room and garage where cars, ambulances and paddy wagons are kept. Afterwards, kids can sit in a courtroom and watch a court in session. Tours are arranged in advance, so reservations are necessary. Shorter tours can be arranged at a precinct station.

Directions: Take Golden Gate Avenue east to Market Street, turn left to 6th Street and right to Bryant.

OAKLAND POLICE DEPARTMENT (Administration Building, 455 7th Street 94607, 273-3069, Officer Cravanas) and the **BERKELEY POLICE DEPARTMENT** (2171 McKinley Avenue, 644-6596, Officer Gaebe) welcome groups of 10 to 15 kids on 45-minute tours of their buildings. Reservations must be made in advance.

Oakland tours are conducted at 9 am, Monday through Friday, during the school year only, for fifth graders and up. Appointments are made by writing to the Chief of Police.

Berkeley conducts its tours year round, 8 am to 4 pm, Monday through Friday, kindergarten age group on up (tours geared to age group), with families fitted in where possible with an organized group. Both Oakland and Berkeley tours include visits to detective division, crime lab, criminal line-up room, radio communications, rifle range if open, fingerprinting department, patrol division, squad room, a possible visit to the jail anteroom, and the garage. The Berkeley Police Department has a 15-minute explanatory talk before the tour for older groups.

Directions: **Oakland Police Department:** BART 12th Street station. By car, Highway 17 to the Market Street off-ramp. Continue on off-ramp street (5th Street) to Broadway and turn left to 7th Street and Broadway, the Hall of Justice.

Berkeley Police Department: BART Berkeley station. By car, Highway 80 to University off-ramp. Take University Avenue to Grove Street, turn right to Allston Way, right one block to McKinley.

SUNSET MAGAZINE (Middlefield and Willow Roads, Menlo Park 94025, 321-3600, Ext. 314, Mrs. King) conducts a 45-minute guided tour of patios, kitchens where published recipes are tested, and editorial offices. Weekdays only. Write or phone for appointment.

Directions: Bayshore Freeway south to Willow Road, west to Middlefield.

LESLIE SALT COMPANY (7220 Central Avenue, Newark, 797-1820) offers a tour of its plant to children 8 or over on Tuesday or Thursday at 10:30 am and 3 pm. After viewing a film on how salt is harvested, you can visit the pressing, packaging, and seasoning areas.

Directions: Highway 17 south to Thornton Avenue exit, west to Cedar Boulevard, south to Central Avenue, then west to plant.

GOLDEN GATE FORTUNE COOKIE COMPANY (23 Ross Alley, off Grant Avenue, between Washington and Jackson Streets, S.F.) allows visitors to its bakery to watch the dough pour out of the machine and see fortunes inserted into cookies. Open every day 9 am-10 pm.

LAWRENCE RADIATION LABORATORY (East End of Hearst Avenue, U.C. Berkeley Campus, 843-2740, Mr. Davenport) conducts year round two-hour tours at 2 pm Tuesday afternoons for junior and senior high school age groups interested in physics and chemistry. The tour begins with a short film explaining research presently taking place at the laboratory, and continues with a trip to the bevatron and control rooms, an explanation of the control panels, then on to the nuclear chemical lab and "water cave," a small room behind walls of water showing the handling of radioactive materials. There's also an interpretation of films showing what happens when accelerated particles collide. Families with young people may make individual reservations for a tour or join an existing group.

Directions: Cross Bay Bridge, take Highway 80 to University Avenue turnoff, east to Oxford, turn left to Hearst Avenue, turn right and drive up hill to Cyclotron Road.

EMBARCADERO — At the foot of Market Street rises the old Ferry Building with the piers and wharves of the Embarcadero on either side, odd-numbered piers on the north and even-numbered piers on the south. This waterfront street, formerly called East Street, parallels the bay shore for three and one-half miles, from China Basin to Fisherman's Wharf.

A number of shipping and cruise lines with ships docked at Embarcadero piers allow visits on board before sailing. Consult a newspaper for ships in port and call the shipper's office downtown. Families are welcome to pick up a pass at the office or, in some cases, passes will be mailed with the date you can board and pier number.

American President Lines, Ltd.
   601 California Street   576-4400

Holland-America Line
   210 Post Street   986-0786

Matson Navigation Co.
   100 Mission Street   982-7700

Pacific Far East Line, Inc.
   1 Embarcadero Center   576-4000

Orient Overseas Line
   311 California Street   981-7340

U.S. NAVAL STATION (Ships Information, Treasure Island, 765-6661) will supply information on the names and types of ships stationed at the naval base, as well as their ship-to-shore telephone numbers. Direct inquiry to any chosen ship will elicit information on tour hours, where ship is berthed, etc. Both individuals and groups are welcome on a guided tour of the naval vessel, which includes an explanation of shipboard routines.

Directions: Bay Bridge to Treasure Island turnoff.

PACIFIC COAST STOCK EXCHANGE (301 Pine Street, S.F., 392-6533) has a visitors' gallery where kids can listen to a 15-minute recorded tape explaining what is taking place on the floor below. Visitors' hours are from 8:30 am to noon, Monday through Friday, suggested grade level 6th and up. Reservations for groups should be made a week or so in advance.

BAY AREA RAPID TRANSIT (800 Madison Street, Oakland 94607, 465-4100, Mr. Rogers) conducts free guided tours of the Lake Merritt facilities 9:30 am-11:30 am and 1:30 pm-3:00 pm, Monday, Wednesday and Friday. The tours include a visit to the automatic train control center where the complicated computer controls are housed, automatic fare collection system, and the train stations. Suitable for children of sixth grade level and up. For group tours, a two-week notice in writing is requested. For individuals, telephone for date of next tour scheduled.

Directions: BART Lake Merritt station. By car, take Highway 17 to Jackson Street off-ramp, south on Fifth Street to Madison, then east on Madison.

TV STUDIOS

The following television studios will arrange tours, by appointment, usually for groups only.

Channel 2, KTVU (1 Jack London Square, Oakland, 834-2000), Tuesdays and Wednesdays at 10 and 11 am. Call promotion department for appointment.

Directions: BART 12th Street station and AC 11, 33, 34, 59 or 76 bus. By car, Highway 17 to Market Street off-ramp. Continue on Fifth Street to Broadway and turn right to Jack London Square.

Channel 4, KRON (1001 Van Ness Avenue, S.F., 441-4444), Mondays and Fridays only, from 9:30 am to noon, for children 13 or over, and in groups of 10 to 20. Call Public Affairs for appointment.

Directions: Take Van Ness Avenue north to Geary.

Channel 9, KQED (525 4th Street, S.F., 864-2000). Call for schedule.

Directions: Take Market Street to Fifth Street and right to Bryant, left on Bryant to Fourth Street.

UNIVERSITY OF CALIFORNIA (Student Union Building, Bancroft Way and Telegraph Avenue, Berkeley 94720, 642-5215, Mrs. Jeffrey) conducts guided one-hour tours of the campus buildings and Sather Tower Monday through Friday, year round except holidays. Groups of 8 or more should call in advance. Individual visitors are welcome to join tour, no appointment needed. Tours start at the Visitors' Center Office in the Student Union Building and visit the lower plaza, Sather Gate, Undergraduate Library, Main Library and the

Tower where, for 10 cents, the elevator takes you to the observation platform for a wide view of the Bay area.

Then to the Physical Sciences Lecture Hall, Lowie Museum of Anthropology, 25 cents for adults, 10 cents for children and, if time permits, a visit to the University Art Museum. Maps and a Walking Guide are also available for self-guided tours.

Directions: BART Berkeley station and AC 40, 51 or 58 bus. By car, take Highway 80 north to University Avenue turnoff, east to Oxford Street, turn right to Durant Street, then left to Telegraph Avenue and left again to Bancroft.

WINE INSTITUTE (717 Market Street, S.F., 94103, 986-0878) will furnish on request its visitors' guide to the California wine country.

San Francisco is the center of five of the major wine-growing regions of America and the world: Sonoma-Mendocino, Napa-Solano, Livermore Valley, Santa Clara-San Benito, and Santa Cruz-Monterey. Over 80 wineries are located within 90 minutes of the city. Most have tasting rooms and some also have picnic tables. Reservations are advised for use of picnic tables or for group tours.

The first vineyards and wine cellars in California, established by Col. Agoston Haraszthy, now a state historical landmark, are located two miles northeast of Sonoma, on Old Winery Road.

All wineries that are open to the public welcome the opportunity and privilege of hosting visitors. Some tours include trips deep into the 100 years or more old storage caves.

Appointments are not usually necessary to visit wineries, but check on major holidays, as some may be closed on these dates.

MUSEUMS, OBSERVATORIES AND PLANETARIUMS WITH SPECIAL ATTRACTIONS FOR KIDS

STEINHART AQUARIUM (Golden Gate Park, 9th Avenue and Middle Drive, S.F., 221-5100) has a dolphin tank, fish from all over world, man-eating piranhas and alligators. Dolphin feeding time is 10:30 am, 12:30, 2:30 and 4:30 pm daily. There's a recording with strange forest noises to make you really feel in the jungle. Open daily 10 am to 5 pm, winter; 10 am to 9 pm, summer. Adults, 50 cents, children, 25 cents, under 12, free. No admission charge on the first day of the month and free admission at all times for organized groups.

Directions: Fell Street to John F. Kennedy Drive; Middle Drive forks to left off Kennedy Drive.

CALIFORNIA PALACE OF THE LEGION OF HONOR (on El Camino del Mar, Lincoln Park, S.F., 558-2881) is an exact replica of its namesake in Paris. It has a permanent collection of 18th century French art. Extensive grounds with a view of the Golden Gate and the sea. Rodin's famous sculpture of "The Thinker" is in the courtyard. Free tours at 2 pm daily. You can lunch at the coffee shop and stay for an organ recital at 4 pm Saturday or Sunday or for special music programs at Christmas and other holidays. Open 10 am to 5 pm daily. Free.

Directions: Van Ness Avenue north to Geary Boulevard, left on Geary to 34th Avenue, right on 34th to park entrance and El Camino del Mar.

M. H. DeYOUNG MEMORIAL MUSEUM (Golden Gate Park, near entrance to 8th Avenue and Fulton Street, S.F., 558-2887) was founded by Michael de Young, publisher of the *Chronicle*, in 1895. In addition to many fine examples of paintings by the Old Masters, tapestries and other decorative arts, the new gallery of the traditional arts of Africa, Oceania and the Americas offers thrilling objects from far-off cultures, well explained with illustrated labels. Everything from a massive Alaskan totem pole to Pre-Columbian gold jewelry. Free tours at 11 am and 2 pm daily. Open daily, 10 am to 5 pm. Free.

Directions: Fulton Street west to 8th Avenue, turn left into park and follow the signs.

SAN FRANCISCO MUSEUM OF ART (corner of McAllister Street and Van Ness Avenue, across from City Hall, S.F., 863-8800) has a small but good collection of modern artists and frequent exhibits of local artists. The museum conducts programs of music and dance for preschoolers through teens, has a teenage animation film workshop, and a free children's film program on some Saturdays at 1 pm. Open Tuesday through Friday 10 am to 10 pm, Saturday 10 am to 5 pm, Sunday 1 to 5 pm. Free, except for special exhibits.

OAKLAND MUSEUM (10th and Oak Streets, Oakland 94607, 273-3401) consists of three major galleries — art, history, and natural science — linked by a series of terraces, gardens and walks in a park-like setting. Free guided tours are conducted Tuesday through Friday at 2 pm. Oakes Observatory multi-media presentation various weekday times. The Natural Science gallery gives kids a simulated walk across California's eight biotic zones. Snack bar and restaurant. Open Tuesday through Sunday, 10 am to 5 pm; Friday night to 10 pm. For tape-recorded time schedules and information on current exhibits and films, dial 273-3585. Free.

Directions: BART Lake Merritt station. By car, Highway 17 to Jackson Street exit, follow 5th Street to Oak Street, then turn left.

UNIVERSITY ART MUSEUM (2626 Bancroft Way, Berkeley, 642-0808) is housed in a handsome modern building, with galleries separated by concrete ramps that go up and down from the main entrance. Tours, by reservation, in which college students lead small groups of 5-10 children in "experiencing" shapes, colors, landscapes, etc. The children do most of the talking. Family art activities three times monthly at the museum or elsewhere in Berkeley. Reservation information: 642-1438. Open 11 am to 5 pm, Wednesday through Sunday. Closed Monday and Tuesday. Free. The museum also has a foreign and art film series. Phone for the program, 642-1124.

Directions: BART Berkeley station and AC 40, 51, or 58 bus. By car, Highway 80 to University exit, turn right to Oxford Street, right on Oxford which becomes Fulton, left on Durant Avenue to College, left on College and left again on Bancroft Way.

AFRICAN AMERICAN HISTORICAL AND CULTURAL SOCIETY (680 McAllister Street, S.F., 864-1010) has a small museum with changing and lively exhibits, including artifacts from Africa, paintings, hammered brass and sculpture, as well as the work of black California artists. Mrs. Elena Albert lectures to groups of school children and other visitors on the early history of blacks in California. Open 9 am to 5 pm weekdays. 12 noon to 4 pm Saturdays. Free.

Directions: Take McAllister two blocks west of Van Ness Avenue.

AMERICAN INDIAN HISTORICAL SOCIETY (1451 Masonic Avenue, S.F., 626-5235) maintains a small museum of American Indian artifacts and a library. Much of the Society's efforts are now directed toward publishing books, but with advance notice tours will be

CHINESE HISTORICAL SOCIETY MUSEUM (17 Adler Place, S.F., 94133) is in the center of Chinatown and its exhibits depict a century of Chinese life and participation in the building of the West. Open daily except Monday and major holidays, 1 to 5 pm. Admission free.

Directions: Van Ness north to California Street, right on California to Grant, left on Grant to Adler which is an alley between Grant and Columbus Avenue just south of Broadway.

FIRE DEPARTMENT PIONEER MEMORIAL MUSEUM (655 Presidio Avenue, S.F.) has a hand pumper from Gold Rush days, wagons, engines, a Fire Chief's buggy, horns, old helmets and fire pictures. Open daily, 1 to 5 pm. Free.

Directions: Van Ness Avenue north to Geary Blvd., take Geary to Presidio Avenue, turn right to 655, which is the corner of Bush.

arranged. Of particular interest to Indian young people as the Director and half the staff are Indian.

Directions: Take Fell Street west, turn left on Masonic.

JUDAH L. MAGNES MEMORIAL MUSEUM, THE JEWISH MUSEUM OF THE WEST (2911 Russell Street, Berkeley, 849-2710) covers 27 centuries of Jewish history and art, including ceramics, costumes, textiles, amulets, and ceremonial objects. Special collections include: materials on Jews in the American West and the gold rush; an exhibit on the Nazi holocaust; and artifacts of Jews in India. Open daily, 10 am to 4 pm, except Saturdays. Free.

Directions: BART Ashby Station and AC 65 bus east. By car, Highway 80 to Ashby exit, right to College Avenue, turn left one block to Russell.

KAISER HEALTH EDUCATION RESEARCH CENTER (3779 Piedmont Avenue, Oakland, 654-4384) offers several educational displays designed to instruct on anatomy, physiology and health habits. Its main exhibit consists of Adam and Eve, the transparent life-sized couple that light up from inside to show the internal workings of the body, while a descriptive taped dialogue is played and colored slides are projected onto a screen. Another exhibit, "The Story of Life," shows the stages of pregnancy from fertilization to birth. Other exhibits deal with dangers of smoking and drug abuse. Open 9 am to 5 pm, Monday through Friday; Wednesday evenings to 8:30 pm, and Sundays, 1 to 5 pm. Closed Saturday. Free. Group tours by reservation: call 645-6571.

Directions: BART MacArthur Station and AC 57 bus. By car, Highway 580 to Broadway, north to MacArthur, turn right to Piedmont Avenue.

ROBERT H. LOWIE ANTHROPOLOGY MUSEUM (Kroeber Hall, University of California, Berkeley 94720, 642-3681) has exhibits on ethnology, archeology and human biology. Open weekdays 10 am to 4 pm, weekends 12-4 pm. Closed major holidays. Admission, 25 cents adults, 10 cents under 12. Professor Lowie, for whom the museum was named, was an authority on the American Plains Indian. A totem pole at the museum's entrance tells the history of a Canadian Indian chief.

Directions: BART Central Berkeley station and AC 40, 51, or 58 bus. By car, Highway 80 to Ashby Avenue exit, east on Ashby to College Avenue, then left to Bancroft Way.

SAN FRANCISCO MARITIME MUSEUM

(Aquatic Park at the foot of Polk Street, 982-1886) transports youngsters back to the early days of San Francisco. It is a nostalgic reminder of an era when square-riggers, down-easters from Maine and Cape Horners were frequent visitors through the Golden Gate. Here are models of the *Preussen*, the first and only five-masted, full-rigged ship built, *HMS Bounty*, and modern super-speed cargo liners. There are mementos of Yankee clippers, early steamers, ferry boats and schooners, and an exhibit of shipwrecks in and around the Golden Gate. Open 10 am to 5 pm daily. Free. Afterwards, walk east to Pier 43, Fisherman's Wharf, where the museum's restored ship, *Balclutha*, a Glasgow-built square-rigger was the last of the fleet that sailed around Cape Horn to San Francisco in the 1880's to load grain from the San Joaquin Valley and jute from Calcutta. Youngsters can see the wheelhouse or the cook's galley, carpenter's shop or fo'c'sle, walk along the decks or sit in the Captain's saloon. Open 9 am to 11 pm daily. Admission: adults $1.50; 12-17 years, 75 cents; under 12, 25 cents; under 6, free.

Directions: Polk Street north to the Bay.

SAN FRANCISCO MARITIME STATE HISTORICAL MONUMENT

(Hyde Street Pier, S.F., 94109, 441-2116) - The sea-scented fog swirls around the four beautifully restored wooden ships berthed at the Hyde Street Pier, and they all seem straining to head out once more into the Bay. There are the side-wheel ferry *Eureka*, in use before the Golden Gate and Bay Bridges were built, with a fascinating collection of automobiles from that era on its lower deck, the steam schooner *Wapama* (with snack bar in the galley), the three-masted sailing schooner *C. A. Thayer*, and the hay scow *Alma*. Kids can board and explore all but the scow. Open 10 am to 8 pm everyday during the summer; the rest of the year from 10 am to 6 pm, Sunday through Thursday; 10 am to 8 pm Friday and Saturday. Adults, 75 cents; 6-17, 25 cents; under 6, free.

Directions: Try this: catch the No. 60 Powell-Hyde cable car at Powell and Market Streets. It will take you up over Russian Hill and down to Aquatic Park, an exciting ride for the kids. By car, take Van Ness Avenue north to Bay Street, then turn right to Aquatic Park.

FERRY BUILDING (at the foot of Market Street, on the Embarcadero) is a San Francisco landmark. Dating from the turn of the century, it survived the 1906 earthquake and its ferries carried thousands of people fleeing the burning city to Oakland. Its tower, 235 feet, was patterned after the bell tower of the Seville cathedral in Spain. The building now houses the California State Division of Mines and Geology (557-0633), with a remarkable exhibit of minerals and rocks, including some real gold nuggets, jade, copper and uranium. Open 8 am to 5 pm weekdays, 10 am to 12 noon on the first Saturday of the month. Here, also, is the World Trade Center, where foreign countries display their goods for sale (wholesale only, but the public is welcome to look) — cars, bicycles, Swedish and German tools, Oriental art objects. Along the ramps are colorful Covarrubias murals of the lands of the Pacific. The building also houses the San Francisco Port Authority, which operates the waterfront. Its public relations office will supply information about the port. Ferries now come and go from an adjacent pier.

ROTARY NATURAL SCIENCE CENTER (Lakeside Park, Perkins Street near Grand

Avenue, Oakland 94612, 273-3739) has films and slide lectures on Sunday afternoons, a nature library, and exhibits of birds and snakes and a beehive with transparent walls. Situated on Lake Merritt, a waterfowl flyway, the Center has lectures on the birds that visit the lake and a daily bird-feeding at 3:30 pm. Summer talks include advice for hikers, campers and vacationers. Times for films and lectures vary, so call for schedule. Open daily 10 am to 5 pm, except Monday. There is also a small junior zoo next to the Center. Animals are fed at 3:30 pm each day. Free.

Directions: BART 19th Street station. By car, Highway 580 to Grand Avenue exit. Turn right on Grand to Perkins and left on Perkins to the Center.

HALLS OF SCIENCE (Golden Gate Park, 9th Avenue and Middle Drive, S.F., 221-5100) house African Hall and North American Hall, with mounted animals and birds in their natural habitats, dinosaurs, and a fascinating collection of clocks and lamps, showing their evolution over the ages. Cafeteria downstairs. Open daily, 10 am to 5 pm in winter, 10 am to 9 pm in summer. Adults, 18 and over, 50 cents, 12 to 17, 25 cents. Under 12 and over 65, and all organized groups free, and also free to all on the first day of the month.

LICK OBSERVATORY (Mt. Hamilton, 408-274-5061) was originally planned for Market Street in San Francisco in the 1870's. Dissuaded by scientists, James Lick, its founder, finally settled on Mt. Hamilton, some 90 miles south of San Francisco. He is buried under its 36-inch refracting telescope. In 1892, the observatory discovered Jupiter's fifth satellite (the first new one since Galileo). A 120-inch telescope, installed in 1959, is the second largest in the world. The long trip, up a steep and winding mountain road (4,200 feet), is well worth it. Open 10 am to 5 pm daily; 12 to 5 pm Saturday and Sunday. Free. For additional information, write to Lick Observatory, University of California at Santa Cruz, Santa Cruz 95060.

Directions: Highway 101 south to San Jose; take Santa Clara Street off-ramp, turn left to Alum Rock where road becomes Mt. Hamilton Road and will take you to the peak.

CHABOT OBSERVATORY AND PLANETARIUM

(4917 Mountain Blvd., Oakland 94619, 531-4560) has a theatre which seats 70, with shows of stars and the heavens Friday and Saturday evenings, 7:30 to 9:30 pm for families and Saturday 1 to 2:30 pm for children. Visitors may also look through the observatory's two telescopes and visit its space science and astronomy exhibits. Adults, 50 cents, children, 25 cents. Call in advance for reserved seats at the show, as this is a popular attraction and attendance is limited.

Directions: Bay Bridge to MacArthur Freeway to Mountain Blvd., turn left to observatory.

ALEXANDER F. MORRISON PLANETARIUM

(Golden Gate Park, 9th Avenue and Middle Drive, S.F., 94118, 221-5100) is one of the best in the United States. It was the first planetarium to install the star projector in its Theatre of the Stars. There are grand tours of the solar system and exploration of the possibility of life elsewhere in space. At the planetarium entrance is the Foucault Pendulum, an ever-popular demonstration of the rotation of the earth. Winter shows daily at 2 pm and Wednesday through Sunday, 8 pm. Extra shows Saturday, Sunday and holidays. Summer shows 12:30, 2, 3:30 and 8 pm. Admission: $1; children under 16 and students, 50 cents. Children under 5 admitted only by special permission. Planetarium open 10 am to 9 pm during the summer, after Labor Day, it closes at 5 pm daily.

Directions: Fulton Street west to Golden Gate Park, turn left into park at 9th Avenue and follow the signs.

CALIFORNIA RAILWAY MUSEUM (Rio Vista Junction, Solano County, 374-2978) has a fascinating collection, in its huge car barn, of old-time rolling stock. Here are, among others, a pair of New York "El" cars built in 1887, a plush observation car from Utah, a classic 1931 solarium lounge car, steam locomotives and street cars of another era. An old-time trolley will take you over 1¼ miles of track, with bell clanging, a unique experience for the young, nostalgia for parents. Admission fee. Trolley cars operate on Saturdays, 12 to 6 pm, and Sundays, 12 to 5 pm, from May through October. (Sundays only, November through April.)

Directions: Highway 80 north to Fairfield, turn right at Highway 12 and drive about 12 miles east to Rio Vista Junction.

EXPLORATORIUM OF SCIENCE, TECHNOLOGY AND HUMAN PERCEPTION (Palace of Arts and Sciences, 3601 Lyon Street at Marina Blvd., S.F. 94123, 563-7337) is a museum with no "Do Not Touch" signs. In fact, youngsters are urged to touch, feel and explore the exhibits and demonstrations, which range from electric music boxes and giant spirographs to music and paintings created by solar energy. There is a maze in a geodesic dome where you bump and slide through various different feeling materials. You can balance a tennis ball on a stream of air, listen to the "Cosmological Harp," or watch patterns produced by your own voice on color TV. The exploratorium is directed by Dr. Frank Oppenheimer, brother of Dr. J. Robert Oppenheimer of atomic energy fame. The museum is fascinating for all ages, but is definitely oriented toward stimulating the scientific interest of young people. Open Wednesday through

Sunday, 1 to 5 pm, and Wednesday nights, 7 to 9:30 pm. Admission free.

Directions: Van Ness Avenue north, turn left at Bay Street which becomes Cervantes Boulevard and runs into Marina Boulevard, left on Marina to Lyon Street.

JOSEPHINE D. RANDALL JUNIOR MUSEUM (199 Museum Way, S.F. 94114, 863-1399) sponsors clubs and study groups of junior astronomers, naturalists, photographers, puppeteers and basket makers, and has kilns and other facilities for making pottery and working in leather and copper, at no charge. Beginning the middle of June and continuing through the summer there are free nature study field trips conducted by the staff. A small zoo in the museum's right wing contains birds, snakes and small animals. On request, the staff will extract a rabbit, guinea pig, or white rat for the children to hold and pet. Send a self-addressed envelope to the museum to receive their summer schedule.

Directions: Market Street west to 15th Street; turn right to Roosevelt Way and then left to Museum Way.

THE LAWRENCE HALL OF SCIENCE (University of California, Centennial Drive, Berkeley 642-5132) is a science education research center with special public programs weekends September through June and daily during July and August. There is a physiology lecture with an automated transparent life-sized model of the human body, lectures on space phenomena, projector slide shows, and experiments to show what science teaching is all about. In between, short films are presented on space, animals, foreign countries, clowns. On weekends year round there are Science Discovery Workshops for children 8-12 years of age which give children an opportunity to observe scientific phenomena that will help them understand the world around them. Register for workshops at Information Desk. Admission: adults $1; children 12 and under, 25 cents. Under 6, free. Group rate is 25 cents per person.

Directions: BART Berkeley station and AC 51 bus, but it's a long walk uphill. By car, Highway 80 to the University Avenue off-ramp and east to Oxford; turn left to Hearst Avenue, then right to Gayley Avenue, left on Gayley to Rimway Road, left to Centennial Drive, and left again to top of the hill.

BANK OF CALIFORNIA OLD COIN AND GOLD EXHIBIT (400 California Street, S.F., 765-2012) is part of the state's history. Founded in 1864, the bank at one time owned a good part of the Comstock Lode. On the bank's lower level is its exhibit of pioneer coins and quartz gold, a million dollar display of "Money of the American West." Open 10 am to 3 pm, Monday through Friday, except bank holidays. Designated S.F. Landmark. Free.

Directions: Van Ness Avenue north to California Street, then right to Sansome Street. The bank is on the northwest corner.

PIONEER HALL (456 McAllister Street, S.F., 861-5278) has an extensive California collection of interesting items from pre-1850 California days. Open 10 am to 4 pm, Monday through Friday. Free.

Directions: Across the street from the Civic Center.

SILVERADO MUSEUM (1347 Railroad Avenue, St. Helena) is north of Vallejo in Napa County and is devoted to the life of Robert Louis Stevenson. For kids who have read and enjoyed his adventure books, *Treasure Island*, *Kidnapped*, or *A Child's Garden of Verses*, the first editions, manuscripts, personal effects, paintings and sculpture will be of interest. Open 12 to 4 pm daily except Mondays and holidays. Free.

FORT POINT (end of Long Avenue, Presidio of San Francisco, 561-3837) lies under the southern end of Golden Gate Bridge. It was built at the time of the Civil War to guard the city of San Francisco from possible attack by sea, and its museum contains old swords, guns, cannons, uniforms, and photos of an earlier day. Kids find it fun to run up and down the stairs, along the parapets or through the arched passageways. Open daily from 1 to 4 pm. Free.

Directions: Van Ness Avenue north to Lombard Street. Turn left to Presidio entrance at Lombard and Lyon Streets. Lombard becomes Lincoln Boulevard inside the Presidio. Follow Lincoln to Long Avenue and Long to Fort Point.

WELLS FARGO BANK HISTORY ROOM (420 Montgomery Street, S.F., 396-2648) re-creates, with photos, documents and mementos, the early days of the West. Vermonter Wells and New Yorker Fargo supplied banking and express services to the gold rush miners. Untold millions in gold and silver were delivered to San Francisco in their six-horse stages. One of the coaches is here, along with the guns used to protect its precious cargo, a mail pouch, posters offering rewards for hold-up bandit Black Bart, bullet-riddled iron doors from the Wells Fargo office in Chinese Camp, and many more exciting mementos from the early West. Open 10 am to 3 pm on banking days. Free.

Very Special Birthday Parties

CASTLE ROCK PARK (1600 Castle Rock Road, Walnut Creek 94598, 934-4569) is a delightful place for teenage parties, although it has many features younger children will enjoy — hayrides, covered wagon ride, two dance pavilions, picnic area, and a variety of sports and games. The hayride, which lasts 1½ to 2 hours, is arranged by reservation only. Group rates are $45 for up to 30 riders and $1.50 per additional rider. A $25 deposit and early reservations are required. The one-hour covered wagon ride, which is great for younger kids, operates weekends and holidays and other times by special arrangement. Group rate is $15 for up to 35 passengers. Smaller groups may join the covered wagon ride, on weekends and holidays only, at 50 cents per passenger.

Juke boxes furnish the music at the two dance pavilions. Activities include swimming, baseball, volley ball, and horseshoe pitching. You may bring your own food to the picnic tables or buy refreshments at the snack bar. Closed, except for weekends, after school starts in the fall. Open weekends again after May 1.

Directions: Bay Bridge to MacArthur Freeway to Highway 24, get off at Ignacio Valley Road, turn right on Oak Grove Avenue which becomes Castle Rock Road, and follow it to the end.

CHILDREN'S FAIRYLAND (Lakeside Park, Grand Avenue and Park View Terrace, Oakland, 444-3510) provides a background for birthday parties of over 50 magical Mother Goose and fairytale characters and settings where children can play and touch. Among the favorites are the Old Woman in a Shoe, Humpty-Dumpty, the Three Little Pigs and, for the more adventurous, a pirate ship to climb on. A minimum fee of $16.75 will provide 12 children with an inscribed birthday cake, candles, ice cream, lollipops, punch, noisemakers, tablecloths, napkins, plates, cups and spoons. Adults may participate. Each additional person, $1.37. A train ride and merry-go-round are nearby and can be included in the birthday celebration.

Puppet shows by Lewis Mahlmann, world-famed puppeteer, are an added feature each day Fairyland is open. Shows are at 11 am, and 2 and 4 pm. Fairyland schedule is: open daily 10 am to 5:30 pm in summer vacation; Wednesday through Sunday, 10 am—5:30 pm, March to June and September to November; weekends and school holidays only, 10 am—4:30 pm, November through February. Admission to park: adults, 60 cents; 1 through 12, 35 cents; under 1, free.

Directions: BART 19th Street station, and AC 12, 18, 34 on Franklin Street (one block over). By car, Highway 580 to Grand Avenue exit, turn right to park.

STORYLAND (S.F. Zoological Gardens, Zoo Road and Skyline Boulevard, S.F., 661-1699) offers delightful birthday parties all year round in a Mother Goose setting among characters such as Old King Cole and Little Red Riding Hood and the Wolf. When weather permits, the parties are held outdoors, and on cold, foggy or rainy days, in the nearby auditorium.

Storyland birthdays include a decorated cake inscribed with "Happy Birthday," the child's name, and the right number of candles; ice cream slices, lollipops, fruit punch, favors, hats, balloons, gay birthday tablecloths, napkins, plates, cups and spoons. An additional attraction is animals children can feed and pet.

Minimum charge $16.80 for 12 children; each additional child, $1.15. Adults may join the party without charge but should bring their own plates and spoons. Reservations must be made at least ten days in advance.

Directions: Highway 280 west to Ocean Avenue. Turn right to Sunset Boulevard, turn right for one block to Sloat Boulevard, then left to Skyline Boulevard.

PEANUTS, THE CLOWN (522-5433) is only 17 years old, but he's the son of a clown and a professional in his own right. He specializes in entertaining the very young — 2 to 5 year old preschoolers. Children particularly like him because he is not too grown up himself. He blows balloon animals, plays with the children, and uses rabbits in his acts which they may hold and pet. Depending upon the attention span, he entertains for 40 minutes to an hour for $20 anywhere in the Bay Area.

RAGGEDY ROBIN, THE MAGIC CLOWN (740-B Shrader, S.F., 751-0217) is a well-known San Francisco clown and mime who comes from an old European circus family and has studied mime in Paris. He will bring his little monkey, Raggedy Joy, to a birthday party, and will grind out tunes on an organ. He also has a magic act with rabbits and doves. He will travel anywhere in the Bay Area; his fee is $40 per party. He also performs for adult functions, PTA and fund-raising affairs. For special events, Robin owns a baby elephant and a baby chimpanzee. RAGGEDY ROBIN'S MAGICAL MIRACLE CIRCUS, a full-length musical about the circus and mostly clowns, but including magicians, jugglers, trapeze artists, a baby elephant, llamas, and chimpanzees, premieres in the spring of 1974. Call for further information.

RAGS, THE MAGIC CLOWN and ROGER MYCROFT, MAGICIAN (522-5432) who are one and the same person, will perform before any age group. Rags, the Clown, is especially good with 4 to 11 year olds. Dressed in his clown suit, he involves his young audience in such amusing make believe as cooking chicken pies which turn into real candy, blowing up animal balloons, telling stories and playing "clapping hands" games. In formal attire, Mycroft, a former circus performer, is a professional magician, with a variety of sophisticated magic tricks for the 12 year olds and up. His fee is $40 for an hour's entertainment, and he will appear anywhere from San Jose to Marin County.

LEONA TROUT POND (4460 Shepherd Street, Oakland, 531-4755) is formed by a natural spring and stocked with rainbow trout. Poles and buckets are supplied free and kids can either flycast or use bait. (Or they can bring their own poles if they prefer.) Admission is free, bait is 10 cents and all you pay for are the fish you catch. There is a picnic area with tables and benches for the birthday party. When the fish are caught they are measured (and cleaned by the attendant if you wish) and you pay according to the size — from 60 cents for a 7-inch fish to $1.30 for 11 inches and over. Open 9 am to 5 pm, seven days a week including holidays.

Directions: BART 12th Street station and AC 15 bus. By car, Highway 580 to Warren Freeway. Take Carson Avenue off-ramp and turn left to Shepherd Street.

ROYAL LICHTENSTEIN QUARTER-RING-SIDEWALK CIRCUS (Father Nick Weber, P.O. Box 4430, San Jose 95126, 408-297-2660) is a three-man circus performing magic, juggling, balancing, escapes and comedy in front of a canvas backdrop. The show has played in 40 states on college campuses, high schools, elementary schools, birthday parties, all for very reasonable fees. Most successful with children's audiences of six years and older. Can be easily performed in backyards, parks or indoors. Write or phone for fees and further information.

HIDEAWAY RANCH (End of Cull Canyon Road, Castro Valley 94569, 581-3141) offers hayrides and a picnic area for birthday parties or other occasions, all year round. The haywagon is pulled by a tractor and costs $1.25 per person. Picnic area is free. Soft drinks are available, but you must bring your own cake and food. Horseback riding is another attraction at $2.50 per hour. Reservations should be made at least one week in advance.

Directions: Bay Bridge to Highway 580 to the Crow Canyon turnoff. Cull Canyon Road is the first left turn off Crow Canyon Road.

BIG OAK STABLES (11425 Cull Canyon Road, Castro Valley 94546, 538-3733) provides horse-drawn hay rides, weather permitting, year round. Its facilities include a barbecue picnic area and a dance floor, making it particularly suitable for teenage parties. Minimum fee is $60 for the first 25 people and $3 per additional person. No charge for picnic area or dance floor. Bring your own food and refreshments. A month's advance reservation is suggested. Open weekends only.

Directions: Bay Bridge to Highway 580 to Crow Canyon turn-off. Cull Canyon Road is the first left turn off Crow Canyon Road.

BERKELEY ICELAND (Ward and Milvia Streets, Berkeley, 843-8800) provides large tables free for birthday parties; you can furnish cake and decorations. For groups of 10 or more, Iceland will give discounts on skate rentals, only if reservations are made in advance. The arena is open all year — mornings: Wednesday and Friday, 10 am to 12:30 pm; Saturday and Sunday, 9:30 am to 12 noon. Afternoons: Tuesday to Thursday, 3 to 5:30; Friday, 3 to 5; Saturday and Sunday, 2 to 5. Evenings: Wednesday and Thursday, 8 to 10:30; Friday, 7 to 10:30 pm; Saturday, 8 to 11, and Sunday, 7:30 to 10. The schedules are changed slightly during school vacations. Rates: adults, $1.50; children 12 to 16, $1.25; under 11, $1. Skates rental 50 cents, with group rates of 35 or 25 cents.

Directions: BART Ashby station, 4-block walk north. By car, Highway 80 north to the Ashby Avenue off-ramp; take Ashby to Grove Street, left on Grove to Ward, and right on Ward to Milvia.

REDWOOD EMPIRE ICE ARENA (1667 West Steele Lane, Santa Rosa, 707-546-7147) will provide birthday parties with a Snoopy theme, as this ice rink is owned by Charles Schulz of "Peanuts" fame. For $32.50, the Arena offers a one-half hour party for ten children, including cake, drinks, a present for the birthday child and favors for all guests. Many of the decorations and favors are based on Snoopy, the world's best known skating dog. Price also includes free skates and skating for the rest of the session. Each additional child, $3.25. On a few special occasions, Snoopy skates at the Arena. Reservations should be made well in advance. Sessions are afternoons: Tuesday and Thursday, 4:30 to 6; Friday, Saturday and Sunday, 2:30 to 5. Evenings: Monday through Thursday, 8 to 10:30; Friday and Saturday, 8 to 11; closed Sunday; Monday, adults only. General admission (included in party rates): children under 12, $1.50; juniors 12 to 17, $1.75; over 18, $2.25. Rates include skate rental.

Directions: Golden Gate Bridge to Highway 101 north to Guerneville Road/Steele Lane exit, drive west and at the third stop light, turn right on Steele Lane.

SAN FRANCISCO ICE ARENA (1557 — 48th Avenue, S.F. 94122, 664-1406) has special rates and rooms for birthday parties. For $25 for the first 10 children, $2 each additional child, the arena will furnish a room, cake, ice cream, soft drinks, tablecloths, napkins, plates, cups and spoons. The fee also includes skate rental and admission for the skating session. Skating sessions all year round at the following hours: afternoons: Monday through Friday, 2 to 5:30; Saturday, 11:30 am to 1:45 pm and 2 to 5; Sundays, 10 am to 12:45 and 1 to 5 pm; holidays, 1 to 5 pm. Evenings: 7:30 to 10:30, except Monday, which is for adults only. During the summer, afternoon sessions on weekdays from 2 to 5.

You can also go to the Ice Arena just for skating. General admission is 75 cents for children under 12 ($1 at night and only if accompanied by an adult); 12 to 16, $1; 17 and over, $1.25. Skate rental, 50 cents. Instruction available and heated snack bar.

Directions: Fell Street west to Stanyan Street, follow Kezar Drive to Lincoln Way, turn right and continue west to 48th Avenue, turn left four blocks.

BUMA, THE MAGICIAN (2242 — 38th Avenue, S.F., 346-2218 or 681-8316) is the owner of the House of Magic, a supply house for magicians, and has himself been a magician for over 40 years. At present, he runs his supply house and is agent for a number of chosen magicians, all bonded and members of the professional organization, International Brotherhood of Magicians. Parents planning a child's or teenager's birthday party can call on him for a suitable entertainer. For a teenage party, he has magicians who entertain with

"ESP" parties, mind reading, fortune telling, astrology, phrenology, palm and tea-leaf reading, as well as sophisticated magic tricks. Fees vary depending on location of party and complexity of apparatus. Give him plenty of advance notice. Kids who want to be magicians themselves, can find all the equipment they need here.

PAUL, THE MAGICIAN (15690 Wagner, San Lorenzo, 278-4311) will entertain at a birthday party for children from 3 to 9 years old with up to an hour show, depending on the attention span of the children. He is a full-time professional, with 25 years' experience. After his magic tricks, which include the top hat and rabbit (which the children may play with), he puts on a 15-minute puppet show with Punch and Judy dolls. His fee is $25 to $35, depending on the distance he must travel. He is a member of the International Brotherhood of Magicians and Jongleurs Circle.

BARRY PUPPET SHOWS (1261 Broderick, S.F. 94115, 922-8787) are the creation of Norman Barry, a well-known Bay Area puppeteer who performs at birthday parties, house parties, picnics, schools and other occasions. The children are involved throughout by talking freely to the puppet and the puppeteer during the show. Fees for private parties, in S.F., $35; for organizations, they will vary according to particular situation. Outside of San Francisco, there is an additional travel fee of $5 in the Bay Area.

LEWIS R. MAHLMANN (700 East 24th Street, Oakland 94606, 839-3078) performs with his puppets at birthday parties when he is not busy putting on shows at Children's Fairyland, Oakland. His program consists of a variety show and the choice of one of four fairy tales. He also performs for schools and organizations. Fee varies with the size and nature of the party.

MILL VALLEY PUPPETEERS (383-0143) will entertain at children's birthday parties. They specialize in folk tales from different lands and cultures. Fees by arrangement. Call several weeks in advance for the Christmas or Easter seasons.

MORNING GLORY THEATRE PUPPET SHOWS (400 San Francisco Boulevard, San Anselmo 94960, 456-8787) are

the creation of Bill Cassady, a professional puppeteer for 15 years, and his wife Mea. They will appear at birthday parties for any age group and put on their own plays geared for the preschooler through 8th grade. Bill and Mea specialize in myths and legends; two favorites are stories from Ghana and East India, both accompanied by music. They will entertain anywhere in the Bay Area. Call for further information and fee.

HIPPO-HAMBURGERS (2025 Van Ness Avenue, S.F., 771-3939) arranges special birthday parties for children in a gallery off the dining room decorated with murals and circus posters. Hippo bibs and lollipops accompany the meal. Waiters serenade the birthday child with

"Happy Birthday to You" out of tune, which the kids love. Hamburgers are, of course, the specialty, with Hippo-, Giraffe-, Rhino-, and Gorillaburgers the favorites. Burgers are 75 cents and up. They also serve "kiddie size" milk shakes. You may bring your own cake or the restaurant will provide one to your specifications. Select an off hour for the party — either before noon or after 1:30 pm, and call for a reservation in advance. Plenty of free parking.

Directions: Van Ness north to 2025.

WINIFRED BRADY (San Francisco, 931-5810) will plan a birthday party for children of any age around a theme suitable to their interests and the group's size. This includes food preparation, decorations, table settings, favors, and entertainment — all to fit the very special interests of the birthday child. Fee dependent on size and type of party.

JEAN A. MANSEAU (865-6911) will help plan, organize and cook for parties for 12-year-olds and up. Jean spent two years in the kitchens of the Waldorf Astoria and can supply the birthday cake as well as anything from hamburgers to an elegant Baked Alaska. He will also secure such entertainment as a magic act or small combo for dancing. Fee depends on size of party, food and entertainment required, but Jean assures that a successful party can be arranged for a relatively modest fee.

THE PRINCESS OF ARGYLE (Bethany Bruno, Honeyhouse, 181 Henry Street, S.F. 94114, 864-0755 or 864-3591) is an unusual storyteller and writer of fairy tales who performs and improvises stories and movements for school groups and community centers, museum happenings, birthday and special occasion parties, as well as libraries, street fairs, video or 'such special royal situations.' Her happenings are created with the help of the participating children, who talk, touch and move together as they improvise. She will entertain at a birthday party and, if you want, she will bring along either a puppeteer (Sharon of Shalimar) or a mime (the Neighborhood Clown), or musicians (Gary Geetar, Robert of Honeyhouse, JoEllen of Melon) 'costumed in the tradition of argylites.' For ages 5 and up. Call Honeyhouse for arrangements and fees.

CLASSES TO DEVELOP TALENTS & HOBBIES

DE YOUNG MUSEUM ART SCHOOL (Golden Gate Park, 8th Avenue and Fulton Street, S.F., 558-3109) has a wide variety of art classes for preschoolers up through the teens in jewelry making, painting, drawing, photography, ceramics, metal arts, sculpture, printmaking, weaving, stitchery, etc. Classes are held in the morning for preschoolers, after lunch for kindergarteners, and after school for older children, as well as Saturday mornings. Call for schedules and fees.

Directions: Fulton Street west from Civic Center to 8th Avenue, turn left into the Park and follow signs.

INTERNATIONAL CHILD ART CENTER (900 North Point, Ghirardelli Square, S.F., 776-7373), besides exhibiting art by children from all over the world year round, conducts art classes for children of nursery school age on up, Tuesday, Thursday and Saturday. For younger children, very simple materials are used: water paints, crayons, clay, etc. Classes for older children include making masques, batiks, etc., as well as painting and drawing. Classes are 1½ hours, once a week, for 10 weeks. Fee is $35 for nonmembers, $30 for members (membership $10). "Glueins" (woodscrap sculpture) are also scheduled from time to time as a whole family activity, adults and children together, on a drop-in basis in the patio.

Directions: Van Ness Avenue north to North Point Street and turn right one block.

SAN FRANCISCO MUSEUM OF ART (4th Floor, War Memorial Veterans' Building, Van Ness Avenue and McAllister Street, 863-8800) has a multitude of programs of music, dance and art for the preschooler through the teens. For the preschooler there is dancing (movement and rhythm) on Saturday mornings and art classes Tuesday mornings and afternoons (10 classes, $30). There are movement and rhythm classes and art and sculpture for ages 5 to 12, Saturday mornings (10 classes $30). Members get a 25% discount on classes.

Directions: This is across the street from City Hall.

ARTS AND CRAFTS PROGRAM (San Francisco Recreation and Park Department, 558-3362) offers a variety of workshops at the Sharon Building, Children's Playground, Golden Gate Park. Classes are open to children and young adults, including a preschooler program. For youngsters, the playground, the most colorful in the city and the oldest in the nation, offers added attractions of a merry-go-round, slides, swings and a cable car to climb on.

Directions: South on Van Ness Avenue to Fell Street. Right on Fell to Masonic Avenue, left to Waller Street and turn right, into the park. Take Kezar Drive which runs into South Drive, and make a sharp right-hand turn into Bowling Green Drive. Park in the lot directly across from the bowling green.

MORRISON PLANETARIUM (California Academy of Sciences, Golden Gate Park, S.F. 94118, 221-5100, Ext. 71) schedules classes in astronomy, for beginners, both adult and children, and other courses such as celestial navigation. For summer and winter schedules phone the planetarium. Class sizes are limited.

Directions: Take Fulton Street west to 8th Avenue, turn left into the park and turn right on Kennedy Drive. Follow the signs to the planetarium.

JOSEPHINE D. RANDALL JUNIOR MUSEUM (199 Museum Way, S.F. 94114, 863-1399) has an auto mechanics class for kids 9 to 14 years on Thursday from 3:45 to 5 pm. The class covers the basic concepts of auto mechanics with emphasis on the working of the internal combustion engine, auto tune-ups and trouble-shooting. Materials fee, $3.50. An Auto Clinic for 16 to 21 year olds is held on Saturday from 1 to 5 pm; materials fee, $3.50. This class is designed for those students needing space, tools and instruction to work on their own cars or motorcycles.

Directions: Market Street west to 15th Street, turn right to Roosevelt Way and left to Museum Way.

PEE WEE BASEBALL is sponsored by the cities of Berkeley, San Francisco, and Oakland from the middle of June through July. Pee Wee baseball is for kids up to 9 years old and teams are formed on most of the city's playgrounds. Kids are introduced to the game and can learn the fundamental baseball skills. For information, call San Francisco 558-3543, Oakland 273-3493, Berkeley 845-1718.

YOUNG AMERICA BASEBALL, OAKLAND is a summer program for all boys, 9 to 15 years, with T-shirt and fully uniformed leagues. Skills training and league play are under professional leadership. Every boy, whatever his skills, plays on a team. Sponsorship is shared by Oakland Parks and Recreation Department (273-3493) and service clubs, business firms, and labor unions.

WARRIOR BASKETBALL CLINICS. Basketball clinics, sponsored by the San Francisco Warriors, are held during the summer in Oakland and South San Francisco. Call Parks and Recreation Departments of Oakland (273-3296) or South San Francisco (588-6200) for locations, dates and times.

BOATING

AMERICAN RIVER TOURING ASSOCIATION (1016 Jackson Street, Oakland 94607, 465-9355) conducts 15-day summer workshops in the fundamentals of kayaking for young people 15 years or older. Beginning on the Stanislaus River, the final expedition moves to Oregon's Rogue River. The workshop objective is to develop competency in safe river touring or in white-water competition. Tuition $450 with a $55 reduction for students who provide their own boat. Write for further details.

U.S. COAST GUARD AUXILIARY (630 Sansome Street, S.F. 556-5310) offers free boating classes in basic seamanship and basic sailing in a wide number of places throughout the Bay Area: Mill Valley, San Francisco, Alameda, Oakland, etc. Most classes start at 7:30 pm and include navigation, charts and compass, boating laws, safe boat handling. Classes are open to both parents and their children. Phone for classes scheduled in your area.

CERAMICS

THE POTTERS STUDIO (2397 San Pablo, Berkeley, 845-7471) offers classes in throwing and hand-building for children 8 to 14 years old, Friday afternoons, at 3:30—5:30. A course of six sessions costs $24. This is a spacious studio with 22 wheels and three kilns where children can learn the potter's art from the mixing of the clay through the glazing process and firing of the kiln. Registration Tuesday nights, 7-9 pm, or call the studio.

Directions: BART MacArthur station and AC 57 bus.

THE MUG SHOP (2925 College Avenue, Berkeley, 548-1425) gives pottery lessons to children from 6 to 12 years of age. Fee $40 for eight lessons, with all materials included.

Directions: BART Rockridge station and AC 51 or 57 bus.

LOUISE A. BOYD MARIN MUSEUM OF SCIENCE (76 Albert Park Lane, San Rafael 94901, 454-6961) sponsors summer classes for young children on the habits and life styles of the animals in the museum's small zoo. The children observe and imitate the animals in games and dances. The museum also has exhibits showing a Miwok Indian village, animals that live in Marin, and other interesting features of the area.

Directions: Highway 101 north to Central San Rafael exit, left on 3rd Street to Lindaro Street, right on Albert Park Lane.

NEIGHBORHOOD ARTS PROGRAM (165 Grove Street, S.F., 558-2335) conducts children's classes in Afro dance and lessons in Swahili. Call for hours and fees.

RIVENDELL SCHOOL (956 Cole Street, S.F., 661-2046), an experimental nonprofit alternative learning center, can, during the regular school year, enroll a visiting child for a 2-week or 2-month stay. Tuition is $150 a month, for children 6 years old to 9. Summer sessions have field trips three times a week and "school" the other two days. It is possible for a child to visit for several days. Call to see if there is space.

Directions: Take Fulton Street, one block west of City Hall, to Masonic Avenue, turn left to Waller Street, right to Cole Street and left on Cole.

LIVE OAK RECREATION CENTER (1301 Shattuck Avenue, Berkeley, 845-1718) has dance, and improvisational exercises based on the theory that dance is a natural and meaningful activity for all young people. Classes are held between the hours of 4 to 6 pm, Monday through Friday, on Saturdays, 9 am to 1 pm. Classes are one hour, once a week, $3; two hours a week, $5; etc.

Directions: Van Ness Avenue between Bush and Pine.

SAN FRANCISCO RECREATION AND PARK DEPARTMENT (Recreational Arts Building, 50 Scott Street, 558-4089, 558-3601) hold free summer children's dance classes as follows. Recreational dance for girls 8 to 13 on Tuesday at 3 pm; modern and Afro dance class on Wednesday, 1:30 pm; modern dance class for girls 16 and over on Tuesday at 7:30 pm;

ballet classes for 5-year-olds (pre-ballet) and 6 through 12-year-olds, weekdays after 3 pm and on Saturdays. Creative dance classes for children 5 years through 15 years are held on weekdays after 3 pm and on Saturdays. Call 845-1718 for specific information on fees and meeting times of the different age groups.

Directions: BART Berkeley station and AC F or 67 bus. By car, Highway 80, to University Avenue off-ramp; take University to Shattuck Avenue, and turn left.

SAN FRANCISCO DANCE THEATER (1412 Van Ness Avenue, S.F., 673-8101) has special children's classes that combine ballet, modern

teen folk and square dance class on Friday at 3:00 pm. All classes are held in the Recreational Arts Building.

Directions: Take Van Ness Avenue to Market Street, turn right to Duboce Avenue, and right again to Scott Street.

YOUNG WOMEN'S CHRISTIAN ASSOCIATION

in San Francisco, Oakland and Berkeley, has a number of dance classes scheduled year round for children and teens. These include Modern Dance (beginning, intermediate, and advanced), Tai Chi Chuan (Chinese calisthenics — movement and meditation in dance form), Hatha Yoga, ballet, Afro-Haitian Jazz Dance, Belly Dancing and, for 3½ to 5-year-olds, Creative Dance. Class fees are between $8 and $12 for eight weeks, depending on the class. Call your local "Y" for dates and hours.

SAN FRANCISCO MUSEUM OF ART (4th Floor, War Memorial Veterans' Building, Van Ness Avenue and McAllister Street, 863-8800) has an animation film workshop for young people 11 to 16. The workshop provides the cameras which the students use to film their story and art work, written and produced during the course. Emphasis is on using animated film as a medium for each student's self expression. Film is provided by the student. Fee for 10 classes, $35 members, $40 non-members. Sessions Saturdays, 1 to 4 pm.

Directions: This is across the street from City Hall.

AMERICAN RED CROSS (1625 Van Ness Avenue, S.F., 776-1500) offers free courses during the year in first aid, as a public service. This is an essential knowledge frequently overlooked, but of more and more value these days. Teenagers should know what to do and what not to do in a crisis of either accident or illness. Classes include filmed demonstrations of skills, programmed workbooks and guided practice sessions. Call your local Red Cross for schedule.

KIDS' GOLF CLINICS are scheduled by the cities of San Francisco, South San Francisco and Oakland during the summer at Harding Park Municipal Golf Course (San Francisco), El Camino Driving Range (South San Francisco), and in 12 different locations in Oakland. Free basic lessons on swing, putting and golf etiquette by professionals are given at Harding Park on three days during July (phone 558-3241 for days); beginning instruction for youths 10 to 17 (6 lessons $12) at El Camino the middle of June to the middle of August, golf balls and clubs provided (phone 588-6200); and free instruction for boys and girls 9 and up of six 1½-hour lessons at 12 different locations throughout Oakland, all equipment furnished. Program ends with a day at Montclair Golf Club or Chabot Golf Course. Parents are welcome to sign up with their children (phone 273-3198).

Directions: For Harding Park, take Fulton Street west from Civic Center to Park Presidio Boulevard, turn left through Golden Gate Park and take 19th Avenue to Sloat Boulevard. Sloat branches left into Skyline Boulevard; take left turn onto Harding Road to golf clubhouse.

To reach El Camino Driving Range, take Bayshore Freeway south to Grand Avenue off-ramp, turn west to 1095 Old Mission Road. Phone for locations in Oakland.

ANTHONY CHABOT EQUESTRIAN CENTER (14600 Skyline Boulevard, Oakland, 569-9830) offers private and group classes in western riding daily from 10 am to 4 pm during the summer months and 10 am to 5 pm during the winter months. Group lessons are $6 an hour, private lessons, $10 an hour; minimum age 7 years old. Anthony Chabot Park has 5,000 acres of park trails for riders. When you call, ask for Tiny Black.

Directions: Highway 580 to Keller Avenue exit, turn left over freeway and continue on Keller to Hansom Drive. Turn left to Skyline Boulevard, then right to 14600.

BOB LORIMER'S OAKLAND RIDING ACADEMY (5745 Redwood Road, Oakland, 531-0262) has classes and private lessons in English riding for 7-year-olds and up, private lessons $10 a half hour, 10 classes (size, about 8 riders), $60. Lessons are given every day and weekends and evenings, Monday through Thursday. Although the Academy has about 50 acres for outdoor riding, most of the classes comprise indoor ring work in riding and jumping. Dressage is also taught but only in private lessons. The Academy's classes may be taken for credit at Mills and Holy Name colleges and are listed as noncredit courses at U.C. Berkeley.

Directions: Bay Bridge to MacArthur Freeway to 35th Avenue-Redwood Road off-ramp, turn left to Redwood Road.

GOLDEN GATE EQUESTRIAN CENTER (Golden Gate Park Polo Field, John F. Kennedy Drive opposite 36th Avenue, S.F., 668-7360) has lessons in English and Western riding for 5-year-olds and up, $7 for an hour lesson, $6

in a class, weekdays 9 am to 4:30 pm. No classes on weekends.

Directions: Fulton Street west to 36th Avenue entrance to Golden Gate Park, turn right into John F. Kennedy Drive and follow signs.

BERKELEY ICELAND SKATING SCHOOL (Ward and Milvia Streets, Berkeley, 843-8803) conducts a hockey clinic in July and August coached by a member of the Oakland Seals. No knowledge of hockey is required but kids must know how to skate. Six 1½-hour lessons for $30 include the basic rules of the game. Clinics coach two age groups: 7- to 12-year-olds and teenagers. The rink is used year round for hockey games at certain hours, and kids 5 years old and up can join teams of their age groups. Iceland also offers skating lessons to kids from 3 years old up, $2 a lesson. Admission to rink: up to 11, $1; 12 and over, $1.25.

Directions: BART Ashby station, 4-block walk north. By car, Bay Bridge to University Avenue off-ramp, right on Milvia Street to Ward Street.

LEGG'S ICE SKATING CENTER (45 11th Street, S.F., near Market and Van Ness, 552-2215) is open year round and conducts a skating school. Lessons for 4-year olds and up are $3.50 a half hour, 5 lessons for $15. Beginners' classes are at 1:30 pm on Saturday. Also figure skating at the same rates. Skate repair and sharpening available. Skate rental is 50 cents.

SAN FRANCISCO ICE ARENA (1557 48th Avenue, S.F., 664-1406) is also open year round and is more convenient for kids living in the west end. The arena is one block from the beach, three blocks south of Golden Gate Park. Class rates are $7 for four lessons on Monday and Wednesday afternoons and Saturday mornings.

REDWOOD EMPIRE ICE ARENA (1667 W. Steele Lane, Santa Rosa, 707-546-7147) gives ice skating instruction to children 10 and under every Friday from 1:15 to 2:15 pm and every Sunday from 1 to 2:30 pm. Fee of $1.50 includes the half-hour lesson, skate rental and free skating for the balance of the session.

Directions: Golden Gate Bridge to Highway 101, north to Coddingtown exit, drive west and at the third stoplight, turn right on Steele Lane.

MUSIC-RECREATION PROGRAM (Oakland Parks and Recreation Department, 569-6418) has a six-weeks summer program from the end of June through the first week of August, combining instrumental music instruction (4th grade through junior high musicians) and arts and crafts instruction. There are playground activities included for those times when the creative spirit lags. Call for information on days and hours.

CAZADERO MUSIC CAMP (17345 Cazadero Highway, Cazadero, operated by the City of Berkeley, 1835 Allston Way, 94704, 644-6520) offers four two-week training sessions during the summer (grades 6 through 12) for talented young musicians in band, chorus, orchestra, ensemble, theory, appreciation, group and private instruction. Artists from colleges, universities, schools and the San Francisco Symphony make up the staff. Cazadero is north of the Russian River in the redwood country (about a two-hour drive north of San Francisco). Students sleep in tents or dormitories and swim, canoe and hike for recreation. Fee for Berkeley residents is $134.50, non-residents $149.50 per session. Partial scholarships available. Fee includes instruction, room, board, supervision, recreational and social activities, films and concerts, health and accident insurance. Phone for additional information. Applications should be in by January 1 of each year.

Directions: Cross the Golden Gate Bridge and take Highway 101 through Santa Rosa approximately four miles to the River Road (Fulton) exit, then take State Route 116 through Guerneville to Cazadero. Visitors are welcome on weekends. Moderate room and board rates.

COMMUNITY MUSIC CENTER (544 Capp Street, S.F., 647-6015) has a wide variety of musical programs starting with beginning group music (Orff method) for children from 4 to 10. This method allows the child to develop in singing, rhythm, improvisation, movement, playing and reading music and music listening. The Center's newly formed San Francisco Children's Chorus provides first-rate choral training for boys and girls ages 7 to 14, and classes for children continue in the highly successful Chinese Music Workshop. Other class instruction is in theory, sight-singing, body movement, Spanish and Latin American dance and drama (ages over 15). Private classes include piano, guitar, recorder, voice, composition, theory, and all orchestral instruments. Moderate fees vary according to family income. A few benefit concerts at nominal charge are given by the faculty to raise funds for scholarships. There are also free faculty concerts and student recitals. Phone Registrar at Center for class schedules and tuition fees.

Directions: Van Ness Avenue south to 20th Street, turn right one block to Capp and left on Capp.

MUSIC DIVISION (San Francisco Recreation and Park Department, 50 Scott Street, 558-4277) conducts music activities year round free of charge. With sufficient interest and registration, activities in Sight Singing, Teenage Dance Band, Instrumental Ensemble, and Recorder are programmed. Applicants must supply their own instruments, except for Rhythm Band instruments which are provided without charge. The Division also conducts ukelele lessons for kids 7 to 12 and guitar lessons for kids 12 to 16. It sponsors Playground Music Periods, conducted by staff members at many recreation centers, consisting of Action Songs, Folk Songs, Toy Symphony, and Creative Music and Rhythms for primary grade age. To encourage group performance, it supports a Recreational Symphony Orchestra which competent young musicians may join by audition before the conductor, Verne Sellin. While primarily a rehearsal group, the Recreational Symphony gives occasional performances. Phone Music Division for schedules. Free.

Directions: Take Van Ness Avenue south to Market Street. Turn right to Duboce Avenue. Take Duboce to Scott Street and right on Scott.

SAN FRANCISCO BOYS CHORUS (Calvary Presbyterian Church, Jackson at Fillmore, 431-5450) auditions boys 8 to 12 years old with unchanged voices. Applicants must be recommended by their music teacher or choir director. The 25-year-old chorus is not connected with the church, but uses its facilities. Boys are trained in theory and sight singing and pronunciation for songs in foreign languages. Rehearsals are twice a week for 1½ hours, 11 months of the year. The 12th month is a four-week summer camp. Tuition is $150 a year (does not include summer camp), with some scholarships available. Music Director is Edwin Flath.

Directions: Take Van Ness Avenue north to Jackson Street, turn left to Fillmore.

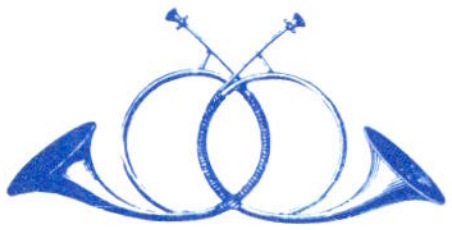

SAN FRANCISCO CHILDREN'S OPERA (245 10th Avenue, S.F., 386-9622) auditions children in the fall for a series of six operas based on fairy tales performed between September and May of each year. Classes take the form of rehearsals for a specific operatic performance. Fees for young participants are $10 per month for ages 5 through 9 and $12 per month for ages 9 up. All youngsters enrolling participate in six fully-staged operettas along with a 20-piece orchestra and a ballet company. Performances are filmed for educational distribution throughout the nation. Phone for fall date of auditions.

Directions: Take Van Ness Avenue north to Geary Boulevard. Turn left to 10th Avenue and then turn right.

SUMMER MUSIC WORKSHOP (San Francisco Symphony Association, 107 War Memorial Veterans Building, S.F. 94102, 861-6240) programs a six-week summer music workshop designed for developing instrumental talent. Open to San Francisco students from private, parochial, and public schools, grades 5 to 12 and jointly sponsored with the San Francisco Unified School District, it operates a workshop with a staff of approximately 32 professional musicians during the first four weeks of the program. The last two weeks are conducted by the 100 members of the San Francisco Symphony Orchestra. Students have the opportunity of learning on a one-to-one basis in band and in orchestra, may participate in conducting laboratory, listening lab, small group ensembles, history, voice, theory and composition. The workshop is free. Phone for registration date and location of workshop.

PHOTOGRAPHY CENTER (San Francisco Recreation and Park Department, 50 Scott Street, 558-4346) has beginner, intermediate and advanced classes in all phases of photography throughout the year. "Quickie" courses in enlarging and printing are given twice weekly and an eight-lecture summer course for beginning photographers is held in the Center during June. Fee is $5 for one year, $3 for six months for students under 19. This membership fee permits, in addition to attending classes, use of darkroom, studio facilities, library, film developing room, and camera club meeting facilities. A free orientation class (required for membership) is held Mondays and Wednesdays at 7:30 pm. An eight-lecture summer course for beginning photographers is held in June.

Directions: Market Street west to Duboce Street, turn right to Scott Street.

SAILBOAT HOUSE, LAKE MERRITT (Oakland Parks and Recreation Department, 568 Bellevue Avenue, Oakland, 444-3807) has sailing classes for children during the summer beginning June 18. Call for hours and tuition.

Directions: BART 19th Street Station and AC 12, 18, 34 on Franklin Street (1 block over) or B buses on Grand Avenue. By car, Highway 580 to Grand Avenue exit, right to Bellevue Avenue.

LAKE MERCED BOAT HOUSE (Skyline and Harding Boulevard, San Francisco, 566-0300, S.F. Recreation and Parks Dept.) gives sailing lessons for beginners and you can get Red Cross certification if you complete the course. Lessons are 9 am to noon on Saturdays, four lessons for $20. Weekday lessons during July.

Directions: Take Market Street and Portola Drive west to Sloat Boulevard, turn right and proceed west to Skyline Boulevard.

MARINER SAILING SCHOOL (Berkeley Aquatic Park, Berkeley, 865-5000) has classes in beginning sailing, Saturdays, 9 am to 1 pm or 1 to 5 pm, Sundays, 9 am to 1 pm. They also have weekday classes year round. Beginning sailing is 20% classroom and 80% on-the-water instruction, learning to rig, dock, run, reach and point. 12 hours, $25. Private instruction is also available if class hours are not convenient.

Directions: BART Berkeley or North Berkeley station and AC 51 bus. By car, Highway 80 north to Ashby Avenue off-ramp to San Pablo, San Pablo to Bancroft and left to Aquatic Park.

MILL VALLEY PARKS & RECREATION DEPT. (180 Camino Alto, Mill Valley, 383-1370) sponsors free canoe and sailing lessons for 12-year-olds and up, given by Mrs. Elizabeth Terwilleger of Mill Valley. Parents are welcome to join the classes also — in fact, Mrs. Terwilleger hopes they will, to make it a family project. There is a fee of $1 for rental of canoe or sailboat. Classes are held in the Mill Valley Small Boat Harbor. Phone or write for schedule.

Directions: Golden Gate Bridge to Highway 101 to Mill Valley turnoff, take Miller Avenue to Camino Alto, turn right.

JOSEPHINE D. RANDALL JUNIOR MUSEUM (199 Museum Way, S.F. 94114, 863-1399) offers year round free classes for young people 9 years old and up from 3:45 to 5 pm, weekdays, Saturday mornings and afternoons. There are classes in beginning chemistry, earth science, ecology, reptiles, Indian lore, seashore life, mineral identification, lapidary, junior naturalists, oceanography, or assisting the museum staff as Museum Aides. Other classes include art, ceramics, textiles, jewelry, weaving, calligraphy and leaded glass. For some, but not for all classes, there is a small materials fee of between $2 and $7. Summer classes are held Monday through Friday, 10 am to noon and 2 to 4 pm.

Directions: Market Street west to 15th Street, turn right to Roosevelt Way and left to Museum Way.

JUNIOR CENTER OF ART AND SCIENCE (3612 Webster Street, Oakland, 655-3226) is a nonprofit, community supported center with low-priced classes in the arts and sciences. Classes are held after school during the week and from 9:30 am to 12 noon on Saturdays. Preschool classes are held in the morning during the week. Twenty-five instructors cover the arts and sciences with puppetry and plays for the preschoolers. Saturday workshops are set up for adult and teenager participation, with no generation gap in the art or harmonica class. Fees for classes are $7.50 for 10 weeks, with chemistry and biology courses higher due to equipment needed. The Center is open 10 am to 5 pm weekdays, 9:30 am to 12 noon on Saturdays. Closed Mondays.

Directions: BART MacArthur station and AC 57 bus to Broadway and MacArthur. By car, Highway 580 to Webster Street off-ramp.

THE LAWRENCE HALL OF SCIENCE (University of California, on Centennial Drive, Berkeley, 642-5132) offers an exciting and unique program of classes for children and adults. Extensive computer courses include creative play with the computer, programming and theory. The instruction is individualized and ranges from beginning topics to advanced ones. In an unusual problem solving course designed to teach some of the skills and strategies involved in problem solving, mysteries, math puzzles and strategy games are explored. Adults and children can both learn about astronomy in the Planetarium classes. Participants learn how astronomy is used to navigate and determine time.

Summer classes also include courses in biology, earth science, photography and chemistry. For six- to eight-year-olds, there is a kitchen science class. In a mineral and gems class, students learn to grind and polish opals. Classes vary from two-week to eight-week sessions. Course fees range from $25 to $50. For further information, call 642-5132.

Summer courses for six- to 13-year olds in outdoor biology are offered by UC's BOTANICAL GARDEN in nearby Straw-

berry Canyon from June through August. Sessions include animal, plant, and horticulture study. Winter programs include a parent-preschool child class on native plants, pond and insect study and ecology. For all ages there's an after-school grow-your-own-garden course. Each student has his own plot, plans his own garden and learns how to tend it. Call Mrs. Ann Wharton for further information, 642-3352.

Directions: Take the Bay Bridge to the University Avenue off-ramp and east to Oxford; turn left to Hearst Avenue, then right to Gayley Avenue, right on Gayley to Rimway Road, left to Centennial Drive, and left again to top of the hill.

LIVE OAK RECREATION CENTER (1301 Shattuck Avenue, Berkeley, 845-1718) has classes in arts and crafts for boys and girls 5 years through 12 years. Children explore different media of materials and emphasis is placed on creativity. Classes during the school year after 2:30 pm. $1 fee per series of classes.

Directions: BART Berkeley station and AC F or 67 bus. By car, Highway 80 north to University Avenue, go east to Shattuck and turn left.

THE SINGER COMPANY has year-round teen sewing classes, eight 2½-hour lessons for $17.50. During the school year, classes are taught in the late afternoon and are small, eight students to a class. Each girl has her own sewing machine, and projects include a dress, suit or coat, depending on her ability to sew. A fashion show climaxes the summer's efforts. For class hours, contact local Singer Sewing Center, or Karen Lewis, Berkeley Singer Co., 841-0446.

instruction for youngsters from 9 to 17 years of age in the Bay Area. Among them are:

MOGUL SKI CLUB (163 Tunstead Avenue, San Anselmo 94960, 453-8844). This club also has special ski classes for youngsters 4 to 8 years old.

HUSKI SKI CLUB (P.O. Box 4267, San Rafael 94903, 472-2121). This club also has summer sailing instruction for young people.

Both ski clubs offer 10 or more Saturday and Sunday one-day trips on winterized charter buses to Sierra resorts. Buses pick up at convenient locations throughout the entire Bay Area. Resorts visited are Boreal Ridge, Alpine Meadows, and Squaw Valley. Fees, depending on the resort, vary from $35 to $75 for 12 Saturday trips, excluding bus fare and lift ticket. The clubs also schedule overnight weekends in the Sierras and out-of-state week-long trips to skiing areas in the Rockies.

SKIING — There are several schools for ski

At **LASSEN VOLCANIC NATIONAL PARK SKI AREA** (P.O. Box 21, Mineral 96063, 916-595-2751) Joe "Rock" McClellan, Director of Ski School, gives free introductory ski instruction twice daily to beginning skiers. The ski shop rents boots and skis. Group rates are $2 per hour, private lessons $5 an hour. (See "Outdoor Adventures.")

CLAIR TAPPAAN LODGE (Sierra Club, Norden, Old Highway 40 near Donner Summit) operates its own ski area with qualified teachers who offer ski instruction to youngsters 9 to 15 years old at a modest fee. The Lodge, $15 per weekend, American plan, provides bunks and mattresses, but guests furnish their own sleeping bags, blankets, towels and outdoor equipment. Quality meals served morning and evening. Special beginners' training sessions are offered for touring, cross-country skiing, and winter mountaineering. Charter bus transportation from San Francisco or Berkeley, weekends only, January through April, $10 round trip. For further information call Sierra Club, 981-8634, Extension 53.

SIERRA CLUB (1050 Mills Tower, 220 Bush Street, S.F. 94104, 981-8634, Ext. 53) offers the beginning snowshoer (16 years old or over) an unforgettable experience in wilderness snow country. With a lodge as home base, there are day-long walks to learn, under expert guidance, how to handle snowshoes under varying conditions. Phone for Sierra Club winter schedule of snow trips (it costs 50 cents). Non-members are welcome to participate.

Directions: Take Van Ness Avenue north to Bush Street, turn right.

COACHES' CAMP OF CHAMPIONS (P. O. Box 1, Moraga 94556, 415-376-5287, Mr. Harless) offers an unusual athletic program to boys 13 to 18 years old. Housed in Stevenson College dormitories on the University of California, Santa Cruz, campus, the campers are provided expert instruction in football, basketball, and baseball by top California college and highschool coaches in these three fields. Instruction includes two hours each morning and afternoon, two hours in the evening, with chalk talks, films, clinics and question and answer periods. Camps run from the end of July to the middle of August, one week for football, one for baseball, and two for basketball. Fees are $105 per week (resident students). $85 per week (day students). Accommodations limited, so apply early.

OAKLAND OFFICE OF PARKS AND RECREATION (1520 Lakeside Drive, 273-3198) has a special summer youth sports program in coordination with the U.S. Coastguard Training Center (boys) and California State University, Hayward, and Laney College (NCAA sponsored, coed), ages 10 to 16. Program includes skills training and competition play in basketball, baseball, football, track, tennis, swimming, gymnastics, archery, modern dance, etc., plus free lunches. Call for information on sign-up procedures.

Directions: BART 19th Street station and AC 12, 18, 34, or B bus.

The Parks Departments of the cities of San Francisco, Oakland and Berkeley all conduct summer swim classes in city pools for 7-year-olds and up. San Francisco classes take place in three outdoor and seven indoor pools (phone 558-3645 for information). Oakland classes are at Live Oak Pool, 1055 MacArthur Boulevard, 273-3494, and Berkeley classes take place in three swim centers. Berkeley, in addition has a Moms and Tots Class, which takes children between 1 and 6 years of age and teaches them how to adapt to the water and learn swimming movements. Parent is in the water with child at all times. Aquatic calisthenics are available in spring, summer and fall, and there are summer classes in skin diving, competitive swimming and water ballet. Phone 644-6530 for information.

City Parks throughout the Bay Area sponsor free tennis lessons at their recreation centers. San Francisco's beginners' tennis lessons are open to children 10 years and older in two-week sessions taught by professional instructors. Outstanding students enter advanced sessions at Golden Gate Tennis Courts. Free. Phone 558-3541 for locations. South San Francisco will take 8-year-olds and up beginning the middle of June for three-week sessions. Phone for locations, 558-6200. For competition tennis training, Oakland offers programs under the direction of the University of California-Berkeley and Cal State-Hayward for boys and girls 12 to 16. Kids 9 through 17, not competition-minded, can register for free instruction. Phone 273-3493. Tennis racquets and balls are provided. Sausalito Parks and Recreation Commission in Marin County conducts free summer tennis lessons at the Martin Luther King Tennis Courts every day for three months during the summer. Kids may take either one of three sessions or all three. More advanced lessons with a professional instructor are five one-hour lessons for $15. Phone 332-1837.

TENNISAMERICA DAY CAMPS (1000 Elwell Court, Palo Alto 94303, 964-4800) are a part of a growing number of summer tennis schools founded by Billie Jean King and Dennis Van der Meer. Bay Area summer camps are in Berkeley (Berkeley Tennis Club) and in San Francisco. Boys and girls 10 to 17 are eligible. Classes feature video stroke analysis, court strategy, and the latest teaching methods.

Trampoline lessons are available year round at some of the recreation centers in both San Francisco and Berkeley. Minimum age 7 years old. Call the San Francisco Recreation and Park Department, 558-4056, or Berkeley Recreation and Parks Department, 644-6530, for locations and hours.

ORGANIZATIONS

SAN FRANCISCO AMATEUR ASTRONOMY SOCIETY (Mr. Armando Zucchi, 474-9006, Secretary) meets every second Friday of each month at 8 pm, at the Josephine D. Randall Junior Museum, 199 Museum Way, S.F. Any serious young student of astronomy from 16 or 17 years up is welcome to attend the membership meetings at which discussions on astronomy take place, with frequent guest speakers. Annual dues are $5, which include a subscription to the monthly magazine *Sky and Telescope*. Members are happy to assist you in making your own telescope, with supplies and tools available through the Society.

Directions: The Randall Museum is reached by going south on Van Ness to Market, west to 15th Street, right to Roosevelt Way and left to Museum Way.

LITTLE LEAGUE BASEBALL, INC. (P.O. Box 1127, Williamsport, Pa. 17701) creates baseball teams of youngsters and through competitive play helps develop good sportsmanship, discipline and leadership through teamwork. A parent — child relationship through the games and practice sessions is encouraged. Regular Little League includes boys age 9 to 12; Senior League, 13 to 15. District Administrator for Bay Area is Theodore J. Sheehan, 2704 Barclay Way, Belmont 94002.

BOYS CLUBS OF AMERICA (Regional Office, 26 O'Farrell Street, S.F. 94108, 781-7588) maintains 23 centers throughout the Bay Area with varied activities for boys from 7-18. Clubs are open afternoons and evenings on weekdays and all day Saturday. Physical fitness activities include basketball, baseball, tag football, tumbling, and boxing. Less strenuous game facilities are available for billiards, checkers, chess, and ping-pong. Arts and crafts activities include drawing, jewelry, lapidary, leatherwork and pottery; fine arts include sculpture, oil painting, choral and instrumental music. The clubs also sponsor special ecology and tutorial programs. Consult your phone directory for club nearest home.

CAMP FIRE GIRLS, GOLDEN GATE COUNCIL (325 Arguello Blvd., S.F. 94118, 752-2600) covers the area of the West Bay counties from Novato in Marin County, through the city of San Francisco, to Menlo Park and East Palo Alto at the San Mateo county line. The smallest members are Blue Birds, 6-8 years old; Camp Fire Girls are 9-11, Discovery Clubbers are 7th and 8th graders, and Horizon Club has as members both boys and girls in senior high. Annual dues are $2 for Blue Birds, $3 for all others. The program emphasizes the individual girl within a small group setting — about 8 to 10 in a group. There is nature study, learning leadership, outdoor experience in group living, either at day camp or resident summer camps. East Bay Councils are: Alameda-Contra Costa Council, 1201 East 14th Street, Oakland, 536-7841; Grizzly Peak Council, 1645 Hopkins Avenue, Berkeley, 524-7556; Piedmont Council, 707 Highland Avenue, Piedmont, 655-7388.

Directions: Take Van Ness Avenue north to Geary Boulevard, turn left to Arguello Boulevard and then right.

CATHOLIC YOUTH ORGANIZATION (1830 Market Street, S.F., 431-1618) sponsors a wide variety of services throughout the Bay Area from nursery schools to retreats for college-age youth. Activities include sports, counselling, employment assistance and social events. Centro Latino (1292 Potrero, S.F.) is a multi-purpose center for the Latin-American community and CYO operates several other programs at centers in the inner-city areas. Archbishop McGucken Youth Center at Occidental, 64 miles north of San Francisco, serves as an all-year center for retreats, conferences, etc., for high school

113

and college age youth. During the summer, it serves as a boys' camp and an adjacent camp is utilized as a girls' camp, open to youth from 7 to 15 years.

4-H CLUBS (Room 162, 224 West Winton Ave., Hayward 94544, 359-0844 [for East Bay], Half Moon Bay, 726-4839 [for West Bay]) are for boys and girls from 9 to 19 years old interested in projects related to agriculture and home economics. Kids might own a horse or cattle, study soil, water, wildlife conservation, train a guide dog, make something out of wood, sew their own clothes, learn automotive care, safety and maintenance, or cook something especially good. Or they might choose engineering or another science project and learn about electricity or small engines. They meet boys and girls with the same interests. There are national and state awards for work in many project areas, and some national awards include college scholarships. There are membership picnics, nature hikes and parties, as well as summer camp. The University of California Agricultural Extension Service also helps with 4-H work and joins with the U.S. Dept. of Agriculture in sponsoring the 4-H program. For information on how to join, call either of the 4-H Clubs above or your county office of the University of California Agricultural Extension Service.

AMERICAN FRIENDS SERVICE COMMITTEE (2160 Lake Street, S.F., 752-7766) sponsors programs to develop youth awareness of social conditions around them. It operates summer volunteer projects such as construction of a building for agricultural workers in the Central Valley or for Indians in Nevada. Work projects in the United States are open to youths of high school age. All volunteers must pay their own travel expenses and nominal room and board. A rural development team in Mexico and similar work projects abroad are open only to college age youth, with participants paying their expenses as well as contributing their services. In a few instances, expenses may be paid by the Friends. Write or phone for brochure "Invest Yourself" which describes work projects in depth.

Directions: Take Van Ness Avenue north to Geary Boulevard. Turn left to 23rd Avenue, right on 23rd to Lake Street.

BERKELEY HIKING CLUB, INC. (P.O. Box 147, Berkeley) is a member of the East Bay Area Trails Council. Annual dues are $3 and $1 more for each additional adult family member. Families with children are welcome, and schedules announce which hikes are easy and which strenuous, so you can tell in advance what age kids should be to join the walk. For additional information, call Club President Lee Sloan, 591-1628.

AMERICAN YOUTH HOSTELS, INC. (625 Polk Street, S.F., 771-9316) sponsors hosteling for all those traveling "under their own steam" — bicycling, hiking, canoeing, skiing, sailing. Northern California hostels are in Calistoga, Mountain Home Ranch; in Los Altos, Hidden Villa Ranch; in Sacramento, Cal-Expo Hostel; and at Pt. Reyes National Seashore. AYH is a membership organization that includes families, teens, college students, and adults. Membership fees are Youth (under 18) $5, Senior (18 and over) $10, Family (including children under 18) $12, organization pass $15. Numerous bicycling day and overnight trips are planned, as well as ski and snow camping trips, horseback rides and sailing. National and international summer cycling trips are also planned. The San Francisco office hours are subject to change. Call office for recorded message. Meetings are held every Thursday from 8 to 10:30 pm at International Institute, 2209 Van Ness Avenue, S.F. Visitors are always welcome.

Directions: Take Polk Street from City Hall five blocks north.

GIRLS SCOUTS OF AMERICA, S.F. BAY COUNCIL (58 Cypress Lane, Brisbane, 467-3330; East Bay: 1400-7th Avenue, Oakland, 834-4844) has scouting programs for girls seven years and older. Members take trips, learn handicrafts, put on plays, help the handicapped, and go camping. Brownies are ages 7 to 8; Junior Girl Scouts, 9 and over; Cadette Girl Scouts, 12 and over; Senior Girl Scouts, 15 and over. The Girl Scouts have day camps and three resident camps at Fairfax, Soda Springs, and Sierraville. Uniforms required.

JUNIOR ACHIEVEMENT (1455 Bush Street, S.F., 776-0252; 866 Estabrook Street, San Leandro) will help boys and girls of high school age set up, incorporate, own, and operate their own businesses under the guidance of adult advisers from business and industry. Some of the business activities sponsored by Junior Achievement include accounting, advertising, manufacturing candles, miniature San Francisco city flags, toys, house number signs, or other products. The program starts in October and ends in April. Groups of 15 are brought together to organize a corporation, which issues shares at $1 each to raise capital. The group elects officers, sets their own salaries and commissions. If the corporation decides to manufacture a product, Junior Achievement has certain machines available. At the end of April, all corporations prepare an annual report and then liquidate. If the corporation has been successful, the shares are redeemed and a dividend not exceeding 20 cents a share is paid. If the corporation operated at a loss, any remaining funds are distributed to the shareholders. Any high school student may join by calling the office nearest home.

Other centers available: San Mateo, Redwood City, South San Francisco, San Rafael, Oakland, and Fremont. For all centers, call 776-0252.

JUNIOR RANGERS (East Bay Regional Park District, 531-9300) is one of the most popular organizations for girls and boys in the Bay area. It is said that parents used to register their sons and daughters at birth as membership is limited. Only about 20 new members are accepted once a year at the beginning of school. Headquarters are in the Tilden Regional Park Nature Area and meetings are held every Saturday during the school year. The Rangers are a nature study group with one-day and overnight hikes an important part of their program. They learn Indian woodcraft and what plants will help them survive in the wilderness. Youngsters 8 or 9 join the Junior Rangers as "Pee-Wees." After a year or so, they become full-fledged Junior Rangers and at 12 or 13 progress to the "Green Shirts." They usually leave at about 14. The "Explorers" accommodate the youngsters on the Ranger waiting list. The program is similar to the Rangers', with hikes, overnight camping and nature study, supervised by the Rangers' Park Naturalist, Paul Ferreira. New members are accepted by the Explorers three times a year — spring, fall, and winter sessions — from ages 6 to 11. Fees: Rangers, $16 a year; Explorers, $4 a session. Phone for registration dates.

THE SAN FRANCISCO ART COMMISSION (558-2335) has set up a Neighborhood Arts Program as a clearing house for information on the many noninstitutional performing arts groups working throughout the city. Their material is frequently ethnic, often experimental. Their stages may be community centers, neighborhood halls and churches, or outdoor parks and squares. Phone to find out what is going on and where at any given time.

BOY SCOUTS OF AMERICA (S.F. Bay Area Council, 8480 Enterprise Way, Oakland, 834-9660; 5228 Diamond Heights Boulevard,

S.F., 647-9509) has a wide variety of activities for boys of all ages. The Cub Scouts (from age 8 or completion of second grade to 11) hold den meetings and simple outdoor activities. Boy Scouts (age 11 or completion of fifth grade through 17) hike, camp, participate in community or conservation services, learn swimming, lifesaving, archery, cooking, nature study, and other useful and exciting skills. Explorers (age 15 or completion of ninth grade to 20) are organized around specialized activities or common career interests such as aviation, electronics, law enforcement, skin diving, or zoology. Many Explorer posts are now co-educational. All groups wear distinctive uniforms and Scout membership includes the privilege of using the many Scout camps maintained by the Council.

To locate the nearest pack, troop, or post, contact either the Oakland or San Francisco offices. If you live outside of San Francisco or the East Bay, consult your phone directory for nearest BSA office.

Directions: Highway 17 to Hegenberger exit, cross over freeway to Edes Avenue, turn right to Enterprise Way. To 5228 Diamond Heights Boulevard, take Van Ness Avenue south to Market Street, turn right and wind around the base of Twin Peaks to Clipper Street which runs off to the left. Take Clipper to Diamond Heights Boulevard.

SIERRA CLUB (National Headquarters, 220 Bush Street, San Francisco, 981-8634) sponsors backpacking, bicycle touring, hiking, mountaineering, skiing, and trail maintenance. It places special emphasis on conservation activities such as preservation of wilderness areas and a clean environment. Maintains mountain lodges. Reference library and files on environmental issues and mountaineering. Membership fees: adult, $15; spouse, $7.50; student (15-23), $8; junior (through 14), $5.

storytelling, and field trips to the zoo, at 9 to 11:30 am. There is also creative movement dancing, 10 hours, $15, and swimming lessons, 8 hours, $20. For older kids, there are winter classes after school and from 9 am to 4 pm, Saturday, in ceramics, chess, cooking, dance, electric workshop, guitar, swimming instruction, beginning tennis instruction (racquets provided), woodworking, judo, karate, puppetry (all materials for classes supplied by Y). Classes range between 75 cents and $2.50 an hour. Horseback lessons are eight one-hour lessons for $35, rental of horses included in fee.

Directions: Fulton Street west to Park Presidio Boulevard, turn left through the park and emerge on 19th Avenue. Take 19th Avenue to Eucalyptus and turn right.

YOUNG WOMEN'S CHRISTIAN ASSOCIATION (620 Sutter Street, S.F., 775-6500) sponsors teen and pre-teen clubs organized for social activities as well as for volunteer service

THE FAR WEST SKI ASSOCIATION (812 Howard Street, S.F., 781-2535) sponsors over 100 races in which more than 1,500 young persons in California and Nevada participate every year. It offers programs for beginners, intermediate young skiers, and for serious racers who want to participate in regional, national and international competitions.

Directions: Take Van Ness Avenue south to Mission Street. Turn left to Fifth Street, right on Fifth and left on Howard Street.

GOLDEN WEST YMCA (333 Eucalyptus Drive, S.F. 94132, 731-1900) has a wide variety of classes for children of preschool age up through the teens, year round. For the 3 to 5 year olds, there are 1½-hour sessions twice a week (10 weeks, $20) with art, music, gym, projects. Pre-teen girls' clubs (ages 9 to 12) go on picnics and camping trips, roller skating and ice skating, have arts and crafts sessions, begin to learn the qualities of leadership. The 12 to 17 year olds in the teen clubs, some of which are co-ed, go on camping trips, hold rap sessions, form drama groups, and learn leadership through involvement in service projects. All clubs have adult club leadership, but are administered democratically by the kids themselves. "Y" classes in dancing, guitar, cooking, art, sewing, etc., are open to all club members. Phone your local "Y" for specific pre-teen and teen programs.

Directions: Take Van Ness Avenue north to Bush Street, right on Bush, right on Mason and right on Sutter Street (these are one-way streets).

WHERE TO TAKE OUT-OF-TOWN VISITORS AND THEIR KIDS

FRONTIER VILLAGE AMUSEMENT PARK (4885 Monterey Road, San Jose, 408-225-1500) features fun and rides with an Old West theme. Added to the 13 customary rides are stagecoach, train and burro rides or canoe trips through Indian country; gold panning and trout fishing. You can also see musical shows and a train robbery. Open summer, Monday through Thursday, 10 am to 5 pm; Friday and Saturday, 10 am to 10 pm; Sunday, 10 am to 7 pm. Winter, weekends and holidays only, 10 am to 5 pm. Closed December 1-25; open daily December 26-January 1. Admission: adults, $2.50; children 4 to 15, $1.50; under 4, free. Single ride, 25 to 50 cents. Discount books available. Admission and unlimited rides for adults or children, $3.50.

Directions: Highway 101 south to Capital Expressway, turn right on Capital Expressway and left at Monterey Road.

ALCATRAZ ISLAND (Harbor Carriers, Pier 43, Fisherman's Wharf, S.F., 396-1141) is now open to the public for the first time since it was ceded by Mexico to the United States in 1848. It first served as a military fort and lighthouse, then as a military prison. It became a federal penitentiary in 1934 and before it was closed in 1963, it housed many notorious criminals. Two of its best known residents were Al Capone and Robert F. Stroud, the "Birdman of Alcatraz." In October 1973, Alcatraz became part of the new Golden Gate National Recreation Area stretching from San Francisco to Point Reyes. You can now take a ferry to the Rock and a walking tour of the island, including the main cell block, conducted by park rangers. Ferries leave every half hour from 9 am to 3 pm and the boat ride and tour will take two hours. Advance reservations recommended. Fares, adults, $2; children 5-12, $1; under 5, free; special rates for groups of 25 or more.

SANTA CRUZ BEACH BOARDWALK AND AMUSEMENT PARK (Beach Street, Santa Cruz 95060, 408-423-7338) offers the best surfing and the largest amusement park in Northern California. Amusements include roller coaster, jet racer and 18 other rides, a penny arcade, and puppet shows. A half-mile boardwalk runs along the beach and amusement park. On the nearby municipal wharf are restaurants, boat rentals, fishing gear and shops. Amusement park rides 30 cents and up, with discount books available. Open year round, except December.

Directions: Take Highway 101 south to Highway 17, then south to Santa Cruz.

SANTA'S VILLAGE (6348 Los Gatos Highway, Scott's Valley, 408-438-2250) contains Santa's home and workshops, elves and animals in a forest setting. A children's amusement park, rides, picnic tables, food, and gift shops are all in the Santa Claus mood. Children can feed baby animals or take an exciting bobsled ride. Open during summer vacations, daily; during the rest of the year, weekends and holidays only, 10 am to 5 pm. Admission: adults, $1.50; children 4 to 16, 50 cents; under 4, free. Rides 35 cents each.

Directions: Highway 101 south to Highway 17, then south to Scott's Valley, seven miles north of Santa Cruz.

MARINE WORLD (Marine World Parkway, Redwood City, 591-7676), an oceanography park, has been combined with Africa-U.S.A. For a single admission, you can see all the shows (allow about five hours) — whales, dolphins, water ski and boat shows, parrots, and over 500 wild animals. Admission covers everything except a boat ride around islands, the canal ride, and the elephant ride, for which there are nominal charges. Admission: adults, $3.90; kids under 12, $2.50. Parking 25 cents. Open every day from mid-May to October, weekends only the rest of the year, from 9:30 am to dusk. Special rates available for schools, Scouts, and other groups.

Directions: Take the Bayshore Freeway south 23 miles to Ralston Avenue exit.

Two of the world's great bridges, the **GOLDEN GATE BRIDGE** and the **SAN FRANCISCO-OAKLAND BAY BRIDGE**, link San Francisco to the north and east shores of the bay. The Golden Gate Bridge, whose 4,200 foot center span was until recently the world's largest, connects San Francisco with Marin County and the north. You can drive or walk its full length (8,940 feet, over 1½ miles) and get marvelous views of the Bay and the headlands as you go. Tolls are southbound only: autos, 50 cents; pedestrians, 10 cents.

The Bay Bridge, which connects San Francisco with the East Bay, is the world's longest steel bridge (8½ miles) and passes through the world's largest vehicular tunnel on Yerba Buena Island. Autos only, toll 50 cents, westbound only.

Other bridges across the Bay, with tolls of 35 cents to $1. round trip, are:

The San Mateo Toll Bridge, about 20 miles south of San Francisco off the Bayshore Freeway, runs from San Mateo to Hayward.

The Dumbarton Bridge, about 35 miles south of San Francisco off the Bayshore Freeway, runs from Menlo Park to Newark.

The Richmond-San Rafael Bridge, about 10 miles north of Oakland (Highway 17).

The Carquinez Bridges (two parallel bridges, each running in a different direction), about 25 miles north of Oakland, from Crockett to Vallejo.

The Martinez-Benicia Bridge, about 40 miles north of Oakland.

CHINATOWN. San Francisco's Chinatown is the largest Chinese community outside of the Asian continent. Its main street is Grant Avenue, running north from Bush Street to Broadway, flanked by narrow streets and alleys running east to Kearny and west to Powell. Grant Avenue, the "street of lanterns," and some of its side streets are lined with restaurants, tearooms, shops, theatres, and markets filled with exotic vegetables and sea plants. There are Buddhist temples and Christian missions, Chinese schools and sweatshops employing recent immigrants.

The architectural style of many buildings, the colorful bazaars, the odor of incense and the lanterns contribute to the Oriental atmosphere. St. Mary's Square, at California and Pine Streets, is dominated by Beniamino Bufano's stainless steel sculpture of Sun Yat Sen, founder of the Chinese Republic, who lived near the square while planning the overthrow of the Manchu rulers. Facing Portsmouth Square, west of Grant from Washington to Clay, are buildings with painted balconies housing Chinese businesses and associations. Your visit should start with a walk along Grant Avenue and a few of its side streets and end at one of its many fine restaurants or tearooms.

Directions: Take Van Ness Avenue north to Bush Street, turn right to Grant Avenue.

CIVIC CENTER (between Franklin and Hyde Streets and Hayes Street to Golden Gate Avenue). A monumental complex of city, state and federal buildings occupies most of the area and is grouped around a plaza. Among the most interesting buildings are City Hall, a French Renaissance structure whose 308-foot dome is taller than the national capitol, and the Opera House, where the founding meetings of the United Nations were held. Others are the Auditorium, the Library, the Federal Office Building, and the underground exhibit area, Brooks Hall.

THE EMBARCADERO, San Francisco's famous waterfront, extends over three miles from Fisherman's Wharf to China Basin. It is lined with piers where you can see passenger ocean liners and freighters from foreign countries, as well as fireboats and ferries from the Bay. On working days you can watch longshoremen loading and unloading. If you're driving, start at Berry Street so you'll be on the bayside of the Embarcadero and can get a better view of the piers.

Across the street, south of Market, is a row of buildings reminiscent of the old days when the waterfront was one of the roughest in the world, and its side streets were called the Barbary Coast. A few saloons and an old hotel are all that remain today, but the word "shanghai", originated in San Francisco and many a sailor, in a bar for a few drinks, ended up on a slow boat to Shanghai. If you're walking, start at Fisherman's Wharf and, if the kids tire, you can stop at the Ferry Building, which is about half way.

Directions: Take Van Ness Avenue south to Mission Street, turn left to Third Street, turn right to Berry Street, then left to the Embarcadero.

FISHERMAN'S WHARF (foot of Taylor Street, off Jefferson Street, S.F.) is the center of San Francisco's colorful commercial fishing fleet. Here you'll see vessels of all sizes, from small crab boats to large tuna ships. On and alongside the wharf are many well-known restaurants and open-air stalls where fresh and cooked crab and other seafood are sold. The wharf is busy at all hours, especially at mealtime.

Directions: Take Van Ness Avenue north to Bay Street, turn right to Taylor Street, left at Taylor to end.

GHIRARDELLI SQUARE (900 North Point Street, S.F.) occupies the old red brick buildings of the former Ghirardelli Chocolate Factory. Terraces overlooking the Bay have been added, as well as fountains, garden patios and a whole fascinating complex of galleries, restaurants and shops. Some of the old chocolate-making machinery has been preserved in the ice cream parlor on the ground floor. A great variety of shops sell materials and crafts from all over the world, as well as American jewelry, tapestries, sandals, and children's toys. The clock tower is a copy of the tower of Chateau Blois in France. Two blocks east, at 2801 Leavenworth, the old Del Monte cannery has been transformed into THE CANNERY, an exclusive shopping and restaurant center similar to the Square, with gardens and splendid views of the Bay. Here are several art galleries, The Cannery Cinema, and, among the restaurants, an authentic Elizabethan pub, the Ben Johnson. Both Ghirardelli Square and The Cannery are open seven days a week.

Directions: Take Van Ness Avenue north to North Point Street, turn right.

NIHONMACHI (an area between Geary and Bush and Laguna and Fillmore Streets) is San Francisco's Japantown. Within this area are Buddhist churches, Japanese movies, restaurants and small stores. Its focal point is the Japanese Cultural and Trade Center at Post and Buchanan Streets with its landscaped Peace Plaza and five-story pagoda. There are shops surrounding the Plaza and lining the bridge over Webster Street, and a theater-restaurant for Kabuki and other performing arts. Public celebrations of Japanese holidays are held in the streets.

Directions: Take Van Ness Avenue north to Geary Street, turn left on Geary and right on Laguna Street.

MISSION DOLORES (Mission San Francisco de Asis, Dolores Street near 16th Street, S.F.) was founded by Father Junipero Serra in 1776 and its buildings were completed before 1795. This unique mission — a composite of Moorish, Corinthian and Mission architectural styles, with adobe walls four feet thick — withstood the earthquake and fire of 1906. The red and white triangular ceiling decorations were painted by the padre's Indian converts. William Alexander Leidesdorf lies buried under the Mission floor and in the little cemetery in back are the graves of former Spanish and Mexican dignitaries. The Mission is open daily, 10 am to 4 pm, November to April; 9 am to 5 pm, May to October. Admission 25 cents, under 12, free.

Directions: Take Van Ness Avenue south to 16th Street and turn right to Dolores Street.

WINCHESTER MYSTERY HOUSE (525 South Winchester Boulevard, San Jose, 408-296-0213) is an incredible maze of 160 rooms with 10,000

windows, 2,000 doors, 47 fireplaces, 13 bathrooms, 50 staircases, blind closets, and secret passageways. It was built over a period of 38 years, ending in 1922, by eccentric heiress Sarah Winchester at a cost of $5 million, to baffle the evil spirits that haunted her. Open daily 9 am to 4:30 pm, except December 25. Admission: adults, $2.50; children 6 to 13, $1; under 6, free.

Directions: Highway 101 south to Highway 17, follow Highway 17 to Stevens Creek exit, right on Stevens Creek and left at Winchester Boulevard.

RIPLEY'S BELIEVE IT OR NOT MUSEUM

(175 Jefferson Street, S.F., 771-6188) has over 500 unusual and bizarre exhibits. One of the more recent displays is a champagne glass through which you can pass your hand, an example of three-dimensional laser photography. Open June 15 through September 15, Sunday through Thursday, 9 am to 11 pm; Friday and Saturday, 9 am to 12 pm; rest of the year, Sunday through Thursday, 10 am to 10 pm; Friday and Saturday, 10 am to 11 pm. Admission: adults, $1.75; children, 12 and under, 75 cents. Educational and group tours by appointment.

Directions: Take Van Ness Avenue north to Bay Street, turn right to Taylor Street, and left to the Wharf.

SONOMA GASLIGHT AND WESTERN RAILROAD

(Broadway, one mile south of the Plaza, Sonoma, 707-938-3912) is a 1/4 scale reproduction of a complete 1890's railroad. The 15-minute trip will take you around curves and up grades, over a high trestle, a 70-foot double bridge, a 50-foot steel girder bridge, and through a tunnel. The ten-acre simulated mountain range is complete with valleys, meadows, trees, and a two-acre lake. There is a three-minute stop at Lakeville, a 1/4 scale meticulous reproduction of historic buildings, including a Wells Fargo express office. Trains leave Train

Town terminal every 20 minutes between 10:30 and 5:30 pm, Saturdays, Sundays, and most holidays, weather permitting. From June 17 to Labor Day, daily except Monday, from 1 to 5:30 pm. Admission 85 cents.

Directions: Highway 101 north to Highway 37, then east to Highway 121, north to Highway 12 which becomes Broadway in Sonoma.

ROARING CAMP AND BIG TREES NARROW GAUGE RAILROAD (Felton, 335-4484) runs south from Felton Station on a one-hour, five-mile round trip. The excursion through the redwood forests of the Santa Cruz Mountains offers awe-inspiring views, dramatic trestles, and spectacular grades. You can stop at Bear Mountain summit to picnic and hike and take another train back. The Red Caboose Diner at Roaring Camp serves hamburgers, hot dogs, ice cream and soft drinks. The 1880 narrow gauge steam train runs daily from mid-June through mid-September and weekends and holidays year round, 11 am to 4 pm. Round trip fare: $3; children 3 through 15, $1.50; under 3, free.

Directions: Highway 35 south to Highway 9, turn right on Highway 9 to Felton.

SEA HABITAT (Fisherman's Wharf, between Piers 39 and 41, S.F.) a two-deck floating aquarium, with displays created by Jean-Michel Cousteau, son of marine biologist Jacques Cousteau, opens in the spring of 1974. According to Cousteau, "People will not only see what is going on in the Bay today, but they'll also be able to look at what has happened to the Bay since it was formed." The lower level will display underwater Bay inhabitants and the upper level will have a 100-seat auditorium and audio-visual exhibits. Watch newspapers for opening date, schedules, and fees.

S.F. MUNICIPAL RAILWAY (949 Presidio Avenue, S.F., 558-4111) has available a Sunday-Holiday tour ticket for 50 cents, good all day long for an unlimited number of rides. The Muni will also furnish a map of tourist attractions and public buildings, with cable car or bus lines which will get you to your destinations. An exciting and inexpensive self-guided tour. You can use the same map and routes weekdays, preferably during the hours of 10 am to 3 pm, at the regular Muni fares (basic fare 25 cents). Sunday-Holiday tour tickets can be purchased from cable car conductors. Write or phone for map or pick it up at the Muni office.

Directions: Take Van Ness Avenue north to Geary Boulevard and Geary west to Presidio Avenue. Turn right.

AC TRANSIT (508 — 16th Street, Oakland 94612, 653-3535; S.F. 434-4334) has operated summer sightseeing tours in the East Bay for several years, visiting such places as Jack London Square, Lake Merritt, UC Berkeley, the Mormon Church, the Coliseum and the Sports Arena. Plans for 1974 are uncertain and we suggest that you check with AC Transit. Meanwhile, you can plan your own tour with the help of AC and BART maps and schedules.

CALIFORNIA STATE AUTOMOBILE ASSOCIATION (150 Van Ness Avenue, S.F. 94101, 565-2711, or nearest local office) will furnish free tour maps of San Francisco to AAA members showing major points of interest and suggested routes, to help you conduct your own guided tour.

Directions: Two blocks south of City Hall.

GRAY LINE TOURS (Depot, 1st and Mission Streets, S.F., 771-4000) provide tours by bus with running commentary on the city's main attractions. Buses leave daily at 10 am, 11 am, 1 pm and 2:15 pm for a three-hour tour. Additional buses, mid-June to late September. Fare: adults, $5.60; children, $2.80. Gray Line also has a bus trip to Chinatown-After-Dark, which includes a walking tour of the area with a Chinese guide. Tours start at 7:30 pm. Adults, $5.50; children 5 to 12, $3.35. From April 1 to November 15, there is also an all-day tour (10½ hours) starting at 9 Monday, Wednesday and Saturday mornings to the Napa Valley and the wine country, including stops at the Christian Brothers winery. Adults, $15.45; children, $10.15, lunch included.

Directions: Take Van Ness Avenue south to Mission Street and turn left to 1st Street.

SF-O HELICOPTER TOURS offer special excursion flight fares for children under 12. The helicopter may be boarded at any of the four heliports of Berkeley, Sausalito, Oakland or San Francisco. The tour takes them to the other three heliports and back, round trip $5.40, 12 years and up, $10.80. The round trip takes about 1½ hours. From S.F. only, there is a special 38-minute excursion flight over San Francisco and the North Bay. Fares: under 12, $3.24; 12 and up, $6.48. Reservations suggested. Heliports to contact for schedules are: San Francisco, TWA Terminal, Gate 53, International Airport, 626-5200; Berkeley, foot of University

Avenue, 845-6816; Oakland International Airport, Earhart Road, Hangar 9, 635-2222; Sausalito, 240 Redwood Highway, 383-3380.

SAN FRANCISCO BAY CRUISE (The Red and White Fleet, Harbor Tours, Inc., Pier 43½, Fisherman's Wharf, S.F., 398-1141) sails from Fisherman's Wharf from 10 am daily, except Thanksgiving and Christmas. Phone for schedule. The 1¼-hour cruise goes under the Golden Gate Bridge, crosses over to Fort Baker, then on to Sausalito, Angel Island, Alcatraz, under the Bay Bridge and then turns and goes back to Fisherman's Wharf. The kids can explore the passageways and decks or listen to a descriptive narration or historical background of what's going by outside. There is a snack bar aboard. Fares: adults, $2.75; children 5 to 11, $1. Children under 5, free.

Directions: Take Van Ness Avenue north to North Point Street, turn right to Mason Street and left to Pier 43½.

TAPE TOURS, which provide portable players and tapes describing major points of interest in San Francisco and how to get to them, are rented for the day by:

Auto Adventures, Fairmont Hotel Lobby, 421-8138, $3.90

Auto Tape Tours, 325 Mason Street, 775-1088, $5

Info Tape, 225 Powell Street, 392-2434, $3.85 and $4.85 for auto tour; $2.85 for walking tour (in Japanese, Spanish, French and German, $3.85)

In addition, there are cassettes with taped descriptions of scenic circuits through Muir Woods, Lake Tahoe, and Yosemite, as well as through San Francisco, which sell for as little as $3.95 and which may be on rental at some Travelodge and Hertz offices. Try the offices nearest you or write Comprehensive Communications, Inc., 565 Fifth Avenue, New York, New York

CHINATOWN WAX MUSEUM (Dupont-Gai Building, California Street and Grant Avenue, S.F., 392-1011) displays 31 dramatic and historic scenes of Old Chinatown and ancient China and over 100 characters in life-like wax. Among the tableaux are a Chinatown butcher shop of the mid-nineteenth century, a fortune cookie factory, a New Year's dragon, and Marco Polo in Kublai Khan's court. The life-size figures are made in Hong Kong. Open daily 10 am to 11 pm. Admission: adults, $1; children 6 to 12, 50 cents; under 6, free.

Directions: Take Van Ness Avenue north to California Street and turn right to Grant Avenue.

THE ENCHANTED WORLD OF OLD SAN FRANCISCO (Jefferson at Mason Streets, 885-4834) is a unique family attraction at Fisherman's Wharf. Visitors ride miniature 1880's cable cars through 14 scenes from the city's past: the Gold Rush, the growth of the city, the great earthquake and fire, New Year in Chinatown, etc. Fun and educational. Open daily Sunday through Thursday, 11 am to 8 pm. Friday and Saturday, 10 am to 11 pm. Adults, $1; children under 13, 50 cents; under 6, free.

Directions: Van Ness Avenue north, turn right at North Point Street, then left at Mason Street.

WAX MUSEUM, FISHERMAN'S WHARF (145 Jefferson Street, S.F., 885-4975) is America's finest and largest, with over 200 life-size figures of statesmen, film stars, criminals and other famous and infamous persons. There are 60 scenes of world leaders and American presidents, a Children's Fairyland, a Chamber of Horrors, and a new Hall of Religion. A former friendly grouping of Chairman Mao, Castro and Kruschev has been dissolved, and President Nixon and the Chinese premier now face each other smiling enigmatically. The Museum is open daily and Sunday, 10 am to 10 pm. Admission: adults, $2; children 6 to 12, $1; under 6, free.

Directions: Take Van Ness Avenue north to Bay Street, turn right to Taylor, and left on Taylor to the end.

OAKLAND ZOO (Knowland Park, 98th Avenue and Mountain Boulevard, Oakland, 569-8819) has performing elephants and an African veldt area, among the many attractions of this small zoo. It also has a Baby Zoo where children may pet and feed young animals (baby goats, hippos, llamas, and dolphin) but only with special food which may be purchased there. A few hundred yards from the Baby Zoo is an amusement area including a miniature train ride, a merry-go-round, ferris wheel, flying saucer, and the Jungle Lift, an aerial tramway for a bird's eye-view of the park. Hamburgers, hot dogs and drinks are on sale at a snack bar. A grassy picnic area among stands of oak is nearby. Admission to zoo, 50 cents a car. Baby Zoo: adults, 75 cents; children 2-14, 50 cents; under 2 and over 65, free. Rides 20 to 35 cents.

Directions: Bart Coliseum Station and AC 56 bus. By car, Highway 580 to 98th Avenue, turn left to Mountain Boulevard.

SAN FRANCISCO ZOO (S.F. Zoological Society, Zoo Road at Skyline Boulevard, S.F. 94132, 661-4844) features reproductions of the natural habitat of animals, separating them from the public by deep moats. The zoo, built by the WPA and modeled after the

Hagenbeck Zoo in Germany, is filled with islands, caves, streams, and waterfalls which give both animals and spectators the illusion of a natural freedom. Among the special attractions are: Monkey Island, with its many caves; elephants in an African Scene, the bear pits, and a tropical walk-through aviary with many nests. There are plenty of picnic tables, a snack bar, gift shop, playground, stroller rentals, free wheelchairs. You can buy a guidebook or a key to "talking boxes" stationed at 40 exhibits, which give descriptions of what you are seeing and will answer children's questions if you are stumped. There's a merry-go-round, miniature train, and other rides, including a 20-minute guided tour on an elephant train.

Feeding hours: lions, 2 pm except Monday; elephants, 4 pm; monkeys, 1:30 pm; leopards and small cats, 2:45 pm. Visitors may buy fish to feed the seals at anytime. Open daily, 10 am to 5:30 pm. Admission to zoo, 50 cents; under 16 and over 64, free; also, certain Tuesdays and Saturdays, free to all. Storyland/Children's Zoo nearby. Admission to Storyland/Children's Zoo: over 15, 25 cents; 14 and under, 15 cents.

Directions: Take Market Street and Portola Drive west to Sloat Boulevard, turn right and proceed west to Skyline Boulevard.

MISCELLANY

OAKLAND A'S BASEBALL CLUB (Oakland Coliseum, Nimitz Freeway and Hegenberger Road, Oakland, 635-4300) offers four "Knothole" days every season to which kids under 14 are admitted free. Apply at any branch of United California Bank (Oakland Main Office, 14th and Broadway, Oakland, 834-8800) and kids will receive a letter of admission and a "Knot-hole Gang" badge. Adult chaperones accompanying kids on Knot-hole days will be admitted for 50 cents each. Seating is on the third deck, where usual admission is $3. On Scout and Little Leaguers Day, not only are the kids in these groups admitted free, but one adult chaperone will be admitted free, too, for each five kids.

There are several family nights when admissions are half-price for all members of the family group. Other special days for kids are Pennant Day, when free pennants are distributed; Bat Day; Cap Day; Helmet Day; and T-Shirt Day, when the free gift matches the name of the day. When the A's play at home on July 4th, there is a fireworks display after the baseball game.

Directions: BART Coliseum station. By car, Nimitz Freeway to the Hegenberger Road off-ramp, cross the freeway to South Coliseum Way.

❧

S.F. GIANTS (Candlestick Park, S.F. 94124, 467-8000) hold a Bat Day at which kids are given bats, a Cap Day at which caps are given away, and a Helmet Day and T-Shirt Day. The Giants also have several free games for kids during the school vacation. Every five kids must be accompanied by one adult chaperone. Apply in writing for an invitation, and check with Giants' promotion department for more complete information.

Directions: Take Highway 101 south to the Candlestick Park off-ramp.

summer, giving as many young people as possible a chance for the job. A referral from the high school job counselor is necessary.

TREASURE ISLAND lies in San Francisco Bay halfway to Oakland by the Bay Bridge. The island was man-made for the 1939 Golden Gate International Exposition and is connected to Yerba Buena Island. It was intended to be used, after the fair, as an airport for San Francisco, but became a naval base in World War II instead. Roads are open 10 am to 4 pm daily, no fee, and offer a view of San Francisco and the Bay. The Bay Bridge passes through a tunnel on Yerba Buena but the off-ramps to this half of the island are closed to the public.

JOBS FOR YOUTH COMMITTEE (Job Coordinator, 1375 University Avenue, Berkeley, 843-1389 or 548-4295) is assisted by the Human Resources Development Center, funded by the Rosenberg Foundation, sponsored by the City of Berkeley Social Planning Dept., and supported by the YMCA, YWCA, and League of Women

AMERICAN FRIENDS SERVICE COMMITTEE (2160 Lake Street, S.F., 752-7766) shares information and discusses with young people alternate life styles, career satisfaction, dress codes, military presence on high school campuses (Jr. ROTC and military recruiters), women's liberation, high school students' rights, etc. Non-sectarian; all young people welcome who may wish to discuss their problems in a group of their peers.

Directions: Take Van Ness Avenue north to California Street, turn left to 23rd Avenue, right to Lake Street and left on Lake Street.

EXPLORATORIUM OF SCIENCE, TECHNOLOGY AND HUMAN PERCEPTION (3601 Lyon Street, S.F., 563-7337), that wonderful spot described under "Museums," where kids are urged to touch, feel and explore the exhibits, pays San Francisco high school students $2 an hour to work as guides after school and during the summer helping visitors use and understand museum exhibits. These "Explainers" are changed after every school term and each

Voters. It calls upon the community to employ its unemployed 13 to 21 year olds who are supervised by competent coaches in gardening, outside work, hauling, house cleaning, appliance repair, typing, babysitting, help for the elderly, dishwashing, etc. Wages, $1 to $2.50 per hour, depending on job skill required and age of workers. Apply to Job Coordinator for after-school, weekend or summer work.

BAY AREA OFFICES OF PARKS AND RECREATION.

Each summer the various Bay Area cities provide work experience for interested high school and college age students who wish to assist in the summer recreation programs. Areas of involvement for students include playground programs, aquatics and park maintenance, working under well-qualified (physical education) Recreation Leaders. Applications for these jobs should be made as early in the year as possible. Some jobs may be volunteer work which will prove an asset for future employment in the area of recreation and some may be salaried but requiring an examination. Information will be supplied by your local Parks and Recreation Department.

OAKLAND PARKS AND RECREATION DEPARTMENT

(1520 Lakeside Drive, Oakland, 273-3494) conducts a year-round evening drop-in gymnastics program at several high school gyms for junior and senior high students; informal workouts under supervision. Summer gymnastics program for all ages at Skyline High. Also year-round instructional gymnastics for junior and senior high girls and summer elementary coed programs. Phone for list of schools where programs take place and for schedules.

"SUMMER JOBS IN FEDERAL AGENCIES"

(at your local post office) is a Federal Government pamphlet with a detailed description of available summer jobs with an application form. Each summer there is a limited number of opportunities for federal government jobs, varying from office positions to park ranger. Early application is necessary. Pick up and the Festival gives them exposure before paid audiences. Judges are drawn from the Oakland and San Francisco symphony orchestras and university music faculties. Auditions take place the end of February or early March, so requests for application cards should be made early each year. William Duncan Allen is Music Director. Audition fee is $3 per instrument.

THE OAKLAND SYMPHONY YOUTH ORCHESTRA

(Paramount Theatre of the Arts, 2025 Broadway, Oakland 94612, 444-3531) offers an opportunity for 60 children of high school age or younger to learn to play before live audiences. Members are selected through audition by Dr. Denis de Coteau, conductor. The orchestra performs throughout the Bay Area and takes an annual national or international tour. For information about applications or specific performances, call manager, Mrs. Ethel London.

Directions: BART 19th Street station. By car, take Highway 580 to Downtown Oakland

brochure in January and apply before February 1.

WORK FOR ALAMEDA YOUTH (1303 Oak Street, Alameda 94501, 522-8400) will help get year round or summer jobs for students from 13 to 18 years of age. Available jobs include baby sitting, bus boy, clean-up work, gardening, and sales. There is no fee for this service which is sponsored by the Alameda Unified School District. Job seekers must fill out applications in person at the agency office.

JUNIOR BACH FESTIVAL (Box 590, Berkeley 94701, 655-6537) was inaugurated 20 years ago in Berkeley. Musicians 18 years old or under may audition and, if accepted, participate in the four or five Bach concerts given every year in the Bay Area. An exception is made for voice, organ or harpsichord for which auditioners may be 20 years old or under. Musicians from as far south as San Diego compete and the standards are very high. Most competitors are pre-professionals exit, continue to West Grand, left to Telegraph Avenue, turn right to 21st Street, then turn right. Entrance is on 21st Street.

SAN FRANCISCO MAIN LIBRARY (Civic Center, 558-3510, Children's Room) — Every second and fourth Tuesday at 4 pm there is a storytelling hour for kids 6 years old and upward, with a special preschool story hour on Tuesdays at 10:30 am. Special events are scheduled in conjunction with such anniversaries as Negro History Week, Cinco de Mayo, as well as the various holidays of the year. Phone for a mimeographed copy of scheduled events. Storytelling hours take place at most of the branch libraries, so check also with your neighborhood branch.

Directions: The main library is directly across the Plaza from City Hall.

THE OAKLAND MAIN LIBRARY (125-14th Street, Boys' and Girls' Room, 273-3166) has a storytelling hour for preschoolers at 10:30 am every Wednesday. Some of the branches also have preschool story hours. Check with your neighborhood branch.

THE BERKELEY MAIN LIBRARY (Shattuck Avenue and Kittredge, Boys' and Girls' Room, 644-6784) has a preschool story hour on Fridays, 10:30 am, followed by a half hour of arts and crafts. Berkeley's four branch libraries also have morning preschool story hours. Call for hours, and also for programs for older children.

SAN FRANCISCO RECREATION AND PARK DEPT. (50 Scott Street, S.F., 558-4089) sponsors a summer storytelling hour for preschoolers up to 12 years old at 1:30 pm Tuesdays in the Sharon Building at the children's playground in Golden Gate Park, off South Drive near the Waller Street entrance. On the first Saturday in May, a May Day program is held in the meadow behind the Sharon Building at 1:30 pm with a Maypole dance, modern dances, children playing ukeleles, and a puppet show. Throughout the summer there are puppet shows and children's plays scheduled at various playgrounds throughout San Francisco. Phone for scheduled dates for these performances. All programs are free.

MAIDEN LANE (off Union Square between Stockton and Kearny Streets) is today one of the most delightful streets in San Francisco. Narrow and only two blocks long, its shops on either side are elegant, modern, and gay. Its history is otherwise. It was the most depraved and infamous red-light district and averaged a murder a week in the 1870's. Burned down in the 1906 fire, it was renamed Union Square Avenue in 1909, Manila Avenue (for Admiral Dewey) in 1921; and in 1922, to show it was really purged of its past, its original name of Maiden Lane was returned to it. There's a pet shop in the Lane that kids can never resist and several places to stop for lunch.

Directions: Take Van Ness Avenue north to Post Street, turn right on Post to the Union Square Garage between Powell and Stockton Streets. Park in the garage and cross Stockton. Maiden Lane starts in the middle of the block between Post and Geary Streets.

COIT MEMORIAL TOWER (on the summit of Telegraph Hill) rises 210 feet from the Hill which is itself 274 feet above sea level and offers from its top one of the finest views over the Bay Area. The sightseeing elevator to the observation floor, 25 cents a trip, runs 11 am to 4:30 pm weekdays, 10 am to 5 pm weekends. WPA murals on the ground floor.

Directions: Take Van Ness Avenue north to Lombard Street and turn right. Lombard ends at Telegraph Hill. Take the winding street to your right, Telegraph Hill Boulevard, to the top.

The following transportation information will be of value to visitors to the Bay Area:

AIRPORTS: San Francisco International Airport, (761-0800), 12 miles south from Civic Center on U.S. Highway Alternate (Bayshore Freeway); Oakland International Airport, across the Bay Bridge, Nimitz Freeway to Hegenberger Road.

DOWNTOWN AIRLINES TERMINAL: O'Farrell and Taylor Streets.

BART (S.F. 788-2278; East Bay 465-4100). Information available in English, Spanish, Chinese, and Braille. Get a copy of the excellent Bart & Buses, Map Guide to Total Transit Travel, available from BART or at stations, hotels, bus depots, chambers of commerce and some banks. Until BART is running under the Bay, AC buses at the Transbay Terminal will take you there — the A bus to Oakland 12th Street station or the F bus to the Berkeley station.

GOLDEN GATE BRIDGE TRANSPORTATION DISTRICT (453-2100 or 332-6600) for information about buses and ferries to Marin County.

SAN FRANCISCO BUSES and STREETCARS: For information call 558-4111. For routes and maps see yellow pages 4 to 8 of telephone directory.

CABLE CARS: Cars leave turntable at Powell and Market Streets for Fisherman's Wharf (Powell-Mason line) and Aquatic Park area, via Russian Hill (Powell-Hyde line). California Street line runs between Market Street and Van Ness Avenue. (558-4111)

GREYHOUND LINES, 7th Street near Market, S.F. (S.F. 433-1500; for other communities consult telephone directory). Service to the Peninsula and other points in the Bay Area.

SOUTHERN PACIFIC DEPOT, Third and Townsend Streets (981-4700), is the station for commute trains from San Francisco to San Jose and peninsula points.

TRANS BAY TERMINAL (AC TRANSIT) First and Mission Streets: Buses to Oakland, Berkeley and East Bay points. (653-3535)

Calendar of Events

CALENDAR

Dates for the following list of annual events change each year, so no dates are given below. In San Francisco, visitors can dial for a day's itinerary. Phone 391-2000 (for out-of-towners, the area code is 415). The 24-hour daily recording provides a two-minute summary of local events and sightseeing tips, courtesy of the San Francisco Convention & Visitors Bureau. For additional information, call the Bureau direct, 626-5500. To check on dates outside of San Francisco, call the local Chamber of Commerce.

Numerous events take place at San Francisco's great exhibit hall, the Cow Palace. Located at Geneva Avenue and Santos Street, it is reached via the Bayshore Freeway, to the Cow Palace off-ramp, turn right on Geneva Avenue. For information, phone 334-4852.

JANUARY

The San Francisco Sports and Boat Show, at the Cow Palace, is the largest sporting exposition in the United States. There is a Huck Finn trout pond for the kids, plus exhibits of vacation equipment and supplies.

Golden Gate Kennel Club All Breed Dog Show, at the Cow Palace, includes more than 2400 dogs and features entertainment. (Or February.)

The San Francisco Examiner Games is an indoor track and field meet held the middle of the month at the Cow Palace.

FEBRUARY

Chinese New Year Celebration, in San Francisco, includes a Chinese Arts and Crafts Fair at the Chinatown YWCA (965 Clay Street), double dragon parade, with block-long Gum Lung (Golden Dragon) and 60-foot-long Hong Kong dragon, ceremonial Lion Dancers, elaborate floats, Kung-Fu demonstrations, folk dancing and singing. Free. Information 626-5500.

Chinese New Year Parade, Oakland, features a children's parade from Lincoln Square Center, 11th and Alice Streets to Jack London Square. Free.

The San Francisco Examiner sponsors the annual **Golden Gloves Amateur Boxing Championships** at the Civic Auditorium, San Francisco.

MARCH

Ski Racing World Series, with top international competitors, is held at Heavenly Valley. For other ski events, call Far West Ski Association, 781-2535.

The San Francisco Annual All-Breed Championship Cat Show is held at the Hall of Flowers, Golden Gate Park.

The Children's Theatre, San Francisco, performs Narzu and the Jungle, March 16, at Presidio Junior High School. Call 982-1333 for time.

St. Patrick's Day Celebration, in San Francisco, features a parade from Montgomery and Bush Streets to the reviewing stand in front of City Hall, plus Gaelic football and hurling contests.

Irish Football and Hurling, Balboa Stadium, Ocean and San Jose Avenues, is an international competition staged in honor of the Irish patron saint. Noisy and lots of fun to watch. Take the 101 Freeway at Franklin Street and Golden Gate Avenue, turn right onto Freeway 280 and off at the Ocean Avenue off ramp.

Bay Area Science Fair, California Academy of Sciences, Golden Gate Park, exhibits science projects by Bay Area junior and senior high school students. Open 10 to 10. Free. (Or April.)

Grand National Junior Livestock Exposition and Horse Show, Cow Palace. The first week of the exposition emphasizes the horse show of hunters, jumpers and Western classes. Only

boys and girls 17 years old and under are eligible to ride. Starts 8 am every morning. The second week continues the livestock exhibit by 4-H Clubs, FFA's, etc., with a livestock auction. Free. (Or April.)

"Spring Comes to Maiden Lane" (just off Union Square) salutes the season with daffodils, spring flowers, and strolling musicians. (Thursday, Friday, Saturday).

Western Stampede, Chowchilla, at the Fairgrounds, features a cattle drive through downtown, steer wrestling, team roping, a barrel race, calf roping. Free. Phone 209-665-3728. Take Highway 101 south to Gilroy, then east on Highway 152 to Chowchilla.

APRIL

Round-Up at Guerneville on the Russian River includes a junior and senior gymkana and barbecue at Birkoffer Field. The gymkana is free. For information, phone 707-226-7736. Take Highway 101 north, turn left onto 116 about 8 miles beyond Petaluma. (Or May.)

Annual Outdoor Easter Sunday Service is held at sunrise on Mt. Davidson, San Francisco's highest point topped by a 103-foot cross.

Easter Sunday Sunrise Service is also held on Mt. Tamalpais, Mountain Theater, Marin County. Take 101 across the Golden Gate Bridge to Highway 1 turn off in Mill Valley to Panoramic Drive.

Easter Egg Hunts are held annually at Children's Storyland/Zoo in San Francisco at 48th Street and Sloat Boulevard, and at the Marin Art and Garden Center, Ross.

The cherry trees in bloom at the Japanese Tea Garden in Golden Gate Park are celebrated in a brief program of dance, music and a visit of the Festival queens in a preview of the Japantown Cherry Blossom Festival below. Free.

A large **Stamp Show**, sponsored by WESTPEX — Western Philatelic Exhibitors — where stamp collectors can buy, trade, look, and learn, is held at the Jack Tar Hotel.

San Francisco Coin Club's coin show is also at the Jack Tar Hotel.

On the opening day of the **Yachting Parade**, in San Francisco Bay, sail and power boats compete for best decorated awards offered by the San Francisco Chronicle. There will be weekend regattas from now until late fall. The best viewing areas are Aquatic Park, Marina Green, and the parking plazas at both ends of the Golden Gate Bridge. (Or May.)

Major League Baseball — the San Francisco Giants at Candlestick Park and the Oakland A's at the Coliseum begin their seasons this month and continue into September.

Apple Festival, Sebastopol, includes gymkana, horse show, a teen dance at 8 pm, a softball game, folk and square dancing. Take Highway 101 north to Highway 116 turnoff between Petaluma and Santa Rosa.

International Sport Cycle Exposition, at Brooks Hall, features extensive representation by motorcycle manufacturers and dealers. Exhibits of custom and antique cycles as well. European Speedway racing, short track races, mini bike races, on a dirt surface in the arena.

Nihonmachi (Japantown) Cherry Blossom Festival (Omatsuri) is held in and around the Japanese Cultural Center at Bush and Buchanan Streets. There are folk songs, a parade, dances, judo and karate demonstrations, flower and bonzai shows, an Akita dog show, ikebana and calligraphy exhibits. Free.

Annual California State Championship Karate Tournament, Civic Auditorium, San Francisco.

MAY

Latin-American Fiesta is a week-long San Francisco celebration that includes a Union Square pageant, a parade in the Mission District, "Cinco de Mayo" program, and dances. Free.

American Indian Pow-Wow, in Hayward, features Indian tribal dances, songs, foods and a handicrafts exhibit. Phone 537-2424.

KQED's annual auction allows a preview showing of the hundreds of items it plans to auction off. Cow Palace. Free. (Or June.)

Mt. Tamalpais Mountain Play, Mountain Theater, Mt. Tamalpais State Park. A very popular annual event in an open air theater and much enjoyed by children. Information, 454-4180.

Napa Valley Horse Show, Foster Road, Napa. Take Highway 101 north to Highway 37, then 121 into Napa.

Shrine Circus, Polack Brothers, Civic Auditorium, San Francisco.

Jumping Frog Jubilee is held at the Calaveras County Fairgrounds, Angels Camp, and features the famous frog jumping competition, a fast draw contest, a rodeo, and a gem and rock show.

Scout-O-Rama is an exposition of scouting by the Boy Scouts of the Bay Area held in alternate years at the San Francisco Cow Palace and the Oakland Arena. In 1974, there will be three separate programs in San Francisco, Oakland, and southern Alameda County. Phone 638-6000 for locations.

Master Mariner's Regatta, San Francisco Bay, is for old style, classic sailing vessels.

Bay to Breakers Cross-City Foot-Race, San Francisco, begins at 10 am, with about 2,000 contestants, on a 7½-mile run through the city ending at Ocean Beach. Prizes for winners.

JUNE

Alameda County Fair, Pleasanton, has a junior exhibit and livestock auction by 4-H Clubs, FAA's and other youth groups. Includes a carnival.

Cross the Bay Bridge, take the Nimitz Freeway to Highway 50, turn south on 680 and take Bernal off-ramp east to Pleasanton.

Livermore Rodeo in Livermore has been a tradition since the early days of this century. A parade precedes the rodeo. Cross the Bay Bridge on Highway 80, take the Nimitz Freeway to Highway 50 which will take you into Livermore.

Solano County Fair, Vallejo, has a carnival, a horse show, plus agricultural and livestock exhibits. Cross the Bay Bridge and take Highway 80 into Vallejo.

Sonoma-Marin Fair, at the Petaluma Fairgrounds, has a rodeo, auto race, a carnival and various exhibits. Cross the Golden Gate Bridge and take Highway 101 north.

Midsummer Music Festival opens at the Sigmund Stern Grove in San Francisco. Free Sunday afternoon programs from the beginning of June to mid-August.

Children's Fair, Boyle Park, Mill Valley. Free. Games, races, puppet shows, pony rides, watermelon seed-spitting contest. Take Highway 101 across the Golden Gate Bridge.

JULY

Fourth of July celebrations and firework displays are held at Candlestick Park in San Francisco, at Larkspur and Corte Madera in Marin County, and at Point Richmond where, in addition, there is a real train ride, a children's parade, and carnival booths. To Larkspur and Corte Madera, go north on 101 to Point Richmond in the East Bay, go north on Highway 80.

Marin Shakespeare Festival takes place at the Palace of Fine Arts, San Francisco, July through September.

Napa County Fair at Calistoga, features livestock, car racing, etc. Take Highway 101 north to Santa Rosa, turn right on Highway 12, left on Calistoga Road and right on Highway 128. (Or August.)

Contra Costa County Fair at Antioch, features livestock and agricultural exhibits, a carnival, etc.

Soap Box Derby has two competitions — at San Jose (408-277-4000) and Vallejo (707-691-1573).

San Mateo County Fair, San Mateo, features horse racing, arts and crafts, and a carnival. (Or August.)

AUGUST

Golden Gateway to Gems is held at the Hall of Flowers, Golden Gate Park.

Livermore Annual Far West Sport Parachute Jump or Sky Diving Meet takes place at the Livermore Airport.

Old Adobe Fiesta in Petaluma features a costume parade, barbecue, milking contest, art show, etc., at 3325 Old Adobe Road. Take Highway 101 north across the Golden Gate Bridge.

Pinole Fiesta, in Fernandez Park, Pinole, includes a street fair, parade, barbecue, etc. Take Highway 80 across the Bay Bridge.

Day of Obon, Japanese Halloween, is celebrated in Japantown, San Francisco, with masques, kimonos, dancing in the streets.

California State Fair at the Sacramento Fair Grounds, has thoroughbred racing, arts and crafts exhibits, a carnival, as well as exhibits of livestock and agricultural products. The big fair of the year. Highway 80 takes you right there. About 100 miles.

SEPTEMBER

Berkeley Art Festival, held at Live Oak or Civic Center Park, has a great variety of handmade articles by ceramicists, jewelry artisans, potters, painters, etc. Free.

Concours d'Elegance, Silverado Country Club, Silverado Trail, Napa. Vintage cars, all lovingly cared for and restored. Prizes for each class. Cross the Bay Bridge and take Highway 80 to the Napa turnoff, Highway 29.

Pageant of Fire Mountain, Guerneville, is an Indian pageant with Indian dances to celebrate Indian Summer. Take Highway 101 north and turn west on 116.

Renaissance Pleasure Faire, Oak Forest, near Novato in Marin County. Take Highway 101 to Highway 37 (the Vallejo exit north of San Rafael), then east one mile to Black Point exit. Admission $3.50, children under 12, $1. Parking free. Wear Elizabethan costumes if you can. The Ha'penny Market offers handicrafts for sale; there are plays, games, jesters, food, and play areas where you can leave the children with competent babysitters when they get tired.

Scottish Gathering of the Clans and Caledonian Games is a tradition over 100 years old. The gathering is at the Santa Rosa Fairgrounds, with pipers, folk dancing, and the famous caber toss. Take Highway 101 north.

Fort Bragg celebrates **Paul Bunyan Days** with a log-rolling contest and parade. About 85 miles north of San Francisco. Take Highway 1 up the coast for a beautiful scenic drive or 101 to north of San Francisco. Take Highway 1 up the coast for a beautiful scenic drive or 101 to Willits and turn west on 20.

Valley of the Moon Vintage Festival in Sonoma, is a famous wine country festival, with band music, dances in the plaza, a parade for children, and a ceremonial blessing of the grapes. Take 101 north, east on 37, and north again on 121 into Sonoma.

OCTOBER

Blessing of the fishing fleet, at Fisherman's Wharf, San Francisco.

Columbus Day Celebration, in North Beach and Aquatic Park, San Francisco, includes a parade and a dramatic representation of Columbus' landing in the western world.

Grand National Livestock Exposition, Horse Show and Rodeo takes place at the Cow Palace.

Marin County Fair in the Civic Center in San

Rafael, runs for four days, with a circus, art exhibit, booths, refreshments, ballet in the evening. Admission $1. Under 6, free. On Highway 101.

NOVEMBER

Dog Show. Northern Dog Days, racing sled dog teams with three-wheeled cart, and a weight pulling contest at Sonoma County Fairgrounds, Santa Rosa.

Black Quake, an exhibit of Black art, films, and theatre at Civic Center Plaza and auditoriums.

The opening of the **Dickens Christmas Fair**, on Hyde and Jefferson Streets, San Francisco. Here you will find food, flowers, handmade toys and giftwares for sale. Fairgoers are encouraged to come in Victorian costumes, top hats and bonnets. Continues through late December.

DECEMBER

The **Shrine East-West Football Game** takes place in Candlestick Park, San Francisco.

Caroling on Lake Merritt has become a tradition in Oakland. A launch can be reserved at Lake Merritt Sailboat House in Lakeside Park for caroling in the evening the week before Christmas. Both launches and listening free.

Children's Christmas Pageant takes place in Oakland Auditorium. Tickets available through Oakland Parks and Recreation Department.

Children's Theater, in San Francisco, schedules two pre-Christmas shows each year in November and December. Call 982-1333 for dates and locations.

Tchaikovsky's **The Nutcracker** plays at the San Francisco Opera House with the San Francisco Ballet, in Oakland at Paramount Theatre with Oakland Metropolitan Ballet, and in San Rafael at the Marin Veterans Memorial Building with the Marin Civic Ballet. Order tickets well in advance.

INDEX

A

Abalone picking 8
AC Transit 131
African-American Historical and Cultural Society 64
Agate Beach 9
Airlines downtown terminal 144
Airports 144
Alameda Beach 10
Alcatraz Island 122
American Friends Service Committee 114, 139
American Indian Historical Society 64
American River Touring Association 34, 91
American Youth Hostels, Inc. 115
Amusement parks 33, 122-124, 135, 136
Angel Island 13, 19-20, 28-29
Animal sculpture 62
Anthony Chabot Equestrian Center 96
Anthony Chabot Regional Park 33
Anthony Chabot rifle range 33
Aquatic Park 8, 31
Audubon Canyon Ranch 34

B

Backpacking 17, 18, 114, 118
Bank of California old coin exhibit 73
Barry Puppet Shows 83
BART 57, 144
• *map* 44
Baseball 90, 108, 112
Baseball, tickets to games 138
Basketball 90, 108, 112
Beachcombing 9, 10
Beaches 9-12, 26, 33
Bear Valley Trails 24
Berkeley Hiking Club 115
Berkeley Iceland Skating School 97
Bicycling 12, 23, 115, 118
• *bikeways* 12-14, 29
• *rentals* 12
Bio-Sonar Laboratory 27
Boating 8, 14, 15, 21, 22, 28, 31, 90
Bob Lorimer's Oakland Riding Academy 96
Bolinas Lagoon 34
Bootjack Campgrounds 16
Boy Scouts 117-118
Boys Club of America 112-113
Brady, Winifred, party planner 85
Bridges 124-125
Briones Regional Park 33
Burna, the Magician 82
Buses 131, 144

C

Cable cars 49, 144
California Railway Museum 71
Camp Fire Girls 113
Camping 16-17, 24, 29
• *winter* 32
Camps
• *summer* 17, 113-120
• *day* 15, 18, 113
• *family* 16
Canoeing 14
• *trips* 18, 115
Castle Rock Park 76
Catholic Youth Organization 113
Cazadero Music Camp 98-99
Centro Latino 113
Chabot Observatory and Planetarium 70
Children's Fairyland 28, 76-77, 84
Children's Theater Association of San Francisco 42-43
China Beach 11
Chinatown 125
• *tour of* 132
Chinese Historical Museum 65
Circuses 78, 79
Civic Center 126
Clamming 18
Classes
• *acting* 99
• *Afro dance* 92, 93, 94
• *animal study* 92
• *archery* 108
• *art* 88, 104, 119
• *arts and crafts* 89, 98, 105, 112
• *astronomy* 89
• *auto mechanics* 90
• *ballet* 93-94
• *band* 99-102
• *baseball* 90, 108, 112
• *basketball* 90, 108, 112
• *batik* 88
• *belly dancing* 94
• *biology* 105
• *boxing* 112
• *calligraphy* 104
• *canoeing* 103
• *celestial navigation* 89, 91, 103

155

- ceramics 88, 91, 104, 119
- chemistry 103, 105
- chess 119
- Chinese dance 94
- choral singing 100
- computer programming 99, 112
- conducting, symphony 104-105
- cooking 120
- dance 88-89, 93, 94, 99, 101-102, 119
- drama 120
- drawing 88, 112
- dressage 96
- earth science 103, 105
- ecology 104, 112
- electric workshop 119
- film making 94
- first aid 95
- folk dance 94
- football 108, 112
- gardening 105
- golf 99, 100, 119
- guitar 108, 119
- gymnastics 108, 119
- Hatha yoga 94
- horseback riding 96-119
- ice hockey 97
- ice skating 80-82, 97-98
- Indian lore 104
- jewelry 88, 104, 112
- jazz dance 94
- judo 119
- karate 91
- kayaking 104, 112
- lapidary 104
- leaded glass 112
- leather work 88
- metal arts 88
- mineralogy 93, 94, 99
- modern dance 91
- motorboating 90
- motorcycle mechanics 90

- music 88-89, 98-102, 112, 119
- nature study 105
- oceanography 104
- organ 100
- painting 88, 112
- physics 105
- piano 99, 100
- photography 88, 102, 105
- pottery 88, 91, 104, 119
- printmaking 88
- puppetry 119
- recorder 99
- rowing 91
- sailing 8-9, 91, 102, 103
- sculpture 88, 89, 112
- seashore life 104
- sewing 106
- skiing 32, 106-107
- square dance 94
- stitchery 88
- Swahili 92
- swimming 108-109, 119
- tennis 108-110, 119
- textiles 104
- track 108
- trampoline 110
- tumbling 112
- ukelele 100
- voice 99, 100-102
- water skiing 8-9
- weaving 88, 104
- woodworking 119

Clowns 78, 86

Clubs
- animal husbandry 114
- astronomy 72, 112
- baseball 112, 138
- business 116
- camera 102
- camping 113, 115-118
- chess 112

- hiking 18, 23, 114-115
- naturalists 72, 117
- photography 72
- puppertry 72

Coaches' Camp of Champions 108
Coast Guard, classes 91
Coins, Old West 73
Coit Memorial Tower 143
Community Music Center 99
Concerts 28, 36, 38, 63
Covered wagon rides 76

D

De Young Memorial Museum 62-63
- Art School 88
Drake's Beach 11

E

Electrovision Theatre 39
Embarcadero 56, 68, 126
The Enchanted World
  of San Francisco 134
Excursion boats 14, 133
Exploratorium 71-72, 139

F

Fairyland, Children's 28, 76-77, 84
Ferries 19-20, 28-29
Ferry Building 68
Films 36, 39-41, 63, 69, 72-73
Fire Department Pioneer
  Memorial Museum 65
Fisherman's Wharf 8, 127

Fishing   8, 10, 11, 15, 18, 20-22, 29, 33, 79, 118, 122-123
Football   108, 112
Fort Cronkhite Beach   9
Fort Point   74
4-H Clubs   114
Friends of the High Sierra   17
Friends Service Committee   114,139
Frontier Village Amusement Park   122

G

Ghirardelli Square   127
Girl Scouts   116
Gold panning   122
Golden Gate Bridge Transportation District   144
Golden Gate Equestrian Center   96-97
Golf   28, 95
Gray Line tours   132
Greyhound buses   144
Gymnastics   140

H

Halls of Science   69
Hayrides   76, 80
Hiking   12, 13, 15, 18, 23-24, 29, 33-34, 114-115, 118
Hippo-Hamburger restaurant   84-85
Horce racing workouts   30
Horseback riding   12, 23, 28, 33, 80, 115
• *camp*   113
Huski Ski Club   106

I

Ice skating rinks   80-82
Indian mounds   26, 27
International Child Art Center   88

J

Japanese Cultural and Trade Center   128
Japantown   128
Jobs   113, 139-141
Josephine D. Randall Junior Museum   72, 90, 103
Judah L. Magnes Memorial Museum   65
Junior Achievement   116
Junior Bach Festival   141
Junior Center of Art and Science   104
Junior Rangers   117

K

Kaiser Health Education Research Center   66
Kayaking   91
Kite removal   25

L

Lake Anza   28
Lake Chabot   14, 22, 26, 28
Lake Merced   21
Lake Merritt   14, 31
Lake Nicasio   22
Lake Temescal   15, 22, 28
Lakeside Park   28
Lassen Volcanic National Park   32, 107
Lawrence Hall of Science   40, 72-73, 104-105
Legg's Ice Skating Center   97
Leona Trout Pond   79
Libraries, children's programs   36, 142
Lick Observatory   69
Lincoln Park   23
Little League Baseball   112
Live Oak Recreation Center   92-93, 105
Louise A. Boyd Marin Museum of Science   25,92
Lowie, Robert H., Anthropology Museum   65, 66

M

Magicians   78, 82-83
Mahlmann Puppets, Lewis R.   77, 83-84
Maiden Lane   143
Manseau, Jean A., party planner   85
Marine World   123-124
Mariner Sailing School   103
Marionette shows   42, 43
Maritime Museum   8, 67
Maritime State Historical Monument   67
Mill Valley Puppeteers   42, 84
Mission Dolores   128
Mogul Ski Club   106
Morning Glory Theater Puppet Shows   84
Morrison Planetarium   70, 89
Mt. Tamalpais State Park   29, 30
Mountaineering   118
Movies   38-41, 63, 69, 72
Mug Shop   91
Muir Woods   24
Municipal Pier   8, 20
Museums
• *African Hall*   69
• *Afro-American*   64

157

158

- Anthropology 66
- Aquarium 62
- Art 62-64, 88
- Chinese 65
- Clocks and lamps
- Fire fighting 69
- Geology 68
- Health Education 66
- Indian, American 64, 66
- Jewish 65
- Maritime 67-68
- Natural Science 63, 68, 69, 72
- North American Hall 69
- Observatory 69-70
- Old West 62, 63, 65, 73, 74
- Physiology 66
- Railway 71
- Science 71, 72
Music auditions for young musicians
- Junior Bach Festival 36, 141
- Oakland Symphony Youth Orchestra 141
- San Francisco Children's Opera 41, 101
Mycroft, Roger, magician 78

N

Nature studies 10, 25-27, 32, 34, 68, 72, 105, 113, 117
Neighborhood Arts Program 92
Neighborhood Clown 86
New Shakespeare Company 43
Nick Weber, one-man circus 79

O

Oakland A's, tickets to games of 138
Oakland Municipal Band 38
Oakland Museum 41, 63
Oakland Seals Ice Hockey Clinic 97

Oakland Symphony Association Youth Concerts 38, 141
Oakland Zoo 135
Observatories 69, 70
Ocean Beach 10
"Old Wharf" nature programs 10, 25-26

P

Palace of the Legion of Honor 36-37, 62
Pan Toll Campgrounds 16
Paradise Beach 11
Parks 17, 23, 26, 140
Parties, birthday or other 76-86
Party planners 82, 85
Paul, the Magician 83
Peanuts, the Clown 78
Pee Wee Baseball 90
Photography Center 102
Picnic areas 8, 10, 11, 12, 14, 15, 22, 24, 26, 27-29, 33, 76, 80, 135, 136
Pioneer Hall 73
Planetarium 69-70
Playgrounds 27, 98
Plays for children 42-43, 143
Point Reyes National Seashore 12, 16-17, 22-24
Potters Studio 91
Princess of Argyll, storyteller 42, 77, 84, 143
Puppet shows 42, 77, 78, 83-84, 85
Puppeteers

Red Cross classes 94-95
Redwood Empire Ice Arena 98
Redwood Regional Park
Restaurants 84-85, 127
Rifle range 33
Ripley's Believe It or Not Museum 129
Rivendell School 92
River rafting 113
Roaring Camp and Big Trees Narrow Gauge Railroad 130
Rock climbing 30
Rotary Natural Science Center 68-69
Rowing 8, 14
- rentals 8, 14
Royal Lichtenstein Circus 79

S

Sailing 8, 21, 115
- classes 8, 102, 103
- regattas 14, 31, 149, 150
- rentals 9, 14, 31
S.F. Amateur Astronomy Society
S.F. Art Commission, information on performing groups 117
S.F. Boys Chorus 100-101
S.F. Children's Opera 41, 101
S.F. Convention and Visitors Bureau 146
S.F. Dance Theater 93
S.F. Giants, tickets to games 138
S.F. Ice Arena 97
S.F. Museum of Art 39, 63
- classes at 88-89
- film workshop 94
S.F. Symphony Orchestra 36
S.F. Zoo 77, 135
Sand castle contest 10
Santa Cruz Amusement Park 123
Santa Cruz Beach 33
Santa's Village

R

Race courses 30
Raggedy Robin, the Magic Clown 78
Rags, the Magic Clown 78-79
Railways, see Trains

Sea Habitat   130
Seal Rocks   33-34, 122
Sharon of Shalimar, puppeteer   86
Sheik of Tranquility, puppeteer   86
Ships, historic sailing   8
Shooting range   33
Sierra Club   23, 30, 107, 118
Silverado Museum   73-74
The Singer Company   106
Skiing   31, 32, 106, 107, 115, 118, 119
Sky Camp   16, 24
Snowmobiling   31, 32
Snowshoeing   107
Sonoma Gaslight and Western Railroad   128
Southern Pacific Depot   144
Stables, horseback riding   80
Star gazing   32
Steinhart Aquarium   62
Stevenson, Robert Louis   73
Stinson Beach   11
Stock Exchange   57
Storyland   77, 136
Storytelling   85, 86, 142
Stow Lake   14
Streetcars   144
Strybing Arboretum   47
"Summer Jobs in Federal Agencies"   140
Surfing   33
Swimming   8, 10, 11, 15, 26, 28, 76, 118

T

Target shooting   33
Teen Center   13
TennisAmerica   109-110
Terwilleger, Mrs. Elizabeth   25, 103
Tours, free
• Airport   46, 47
• Airport National Weather Service   46

• Arboretum   47
• Baby food factory   52
• Bakeries   48
• BART   57
• Bio-Sonar Laboratory   27
• Cable car barn   49
• Chocolate factory   48
• Churches   49, 50
• Fire Department and Fireboat   51-52
• Heliport   46
• Ice cream factory   52
• Levis factory   50
• Magazine publisher   55
• Museum   63
• Navy ships   56-57
• Ocean liners   56
• Oil industry exhibit   53
• Police department   53-54
• Radiation Laboratory   55-56
• Stock exchange   57
• Sugar refinery   55
• TV studios   58
• University of California, Berkeley   58-59
• Vineyards   59-60
Tour maps   132
Tour portable players and tapes   133
Tours via AC Transit   131
• Gray Line   132
• helicopter   132
• Red and White Harbor Fleet   133
• S.F. Municipal railway   131
• of wine country   132
Trail maintenance   118
Trains   71, 122, 129-130
Transportation information   144
Treasure Island   139
Tripark bikeways   12-13
TV   43, 58

U

U.C. Art Museum   40, 64
U.C. Berkeley   58-59
U.C. Music Department   38-39

W

Warrior Basketball clinics   90
Water-skiing   8
Wax Museums
• Chinatown   134
• Fisherman's Wharf   134-135
Weather, highway conditions information   31
Wells Fargo Bank History Room   74
Whale watching   12, 34
White water rafting   18, 34
Winchester Mystery House   128-129
Wineries   59
Work for Alameda Youth, summer jobs   114
Work projects (Friends)   141
Workshops
• film   94
• music   101
• science   73

Y

Young American Baseball   90
YMCA   18
YMCA - Golden West   119
YMCA - Park Presidio   119-120
YWCA   94, 120

Z

Zoo trips for preschoolers   119
Zoos   77, 135-136
Zoos, children's   69, 72, 135

This book is published by
PRICE/STERN/SLOAN
Publishers, Inc.

whose other splendid titles include such literary classics as:

San Francisco. An Unusual Guide
To Unusual Shopping

The Good News, Bad News Book

The Elephant Book

Elephants, Grapes & Pickles

The Monster Joke Book

Droodles

The World's Worst Jokes

The Mad Libs series

The Designs To Color series

and many, many more

They are available at your bookseller's, or may be ordered directly from the publisher. For complete list, write:

PRICE/STERN/SLOAN

Publishers, Inc.

**410 North La Cienega Boulevard
Los Angeles, California 90048**